Guideposts for The Journey Home

GUIDEPOSTS FOR THE JOURNEY HOME:

Conversion Stories with Marcus Grodi

With an *Introduction* by Marcus Grodi

Edited by Laura Rachel Yanikoski

EWTN PUBLISHING, INC.
Irondale, Alabama

EWTN Publishing, Inc.
5817 Old Leeds Road, Irondale, AL 35210

Distributed by Sophia Institute Press, Box 5284, Manchester, NH 03108.

paperback ISBN 978-1-68278-346-7
ebook ISBN 978-1-68278-347-4
Library of Congress Control Number: 2023952257

First printing

"Set up waymarks for yourself, make yourself guideposts;
consider well the highway, the road by which you went.
Return, O virgin Israel, return to these your cities."
(Jeremiah 31:21)

Contents

Introduction
  by Marcus Grodi. .3

Our Continual Conversion
  Interview with Fr. Benedict Groeschel, C.F.R.
  (August 2007). 5

The Stages of the Spiritual Life
  Interview with Mother Angelica (August 2000). . . . 29

Obstacles to Coming Home
  Interview with Mother Angelica (September 2001). . 53

The Church Is the Family of God
  Interview with Scott Hahn (May 1998). 77

The Church Is the Kingdom of God
  Interview with Scott Hahn (September 1999). . . . 103

The Sacramental Basis of Our Hope
  Interview with Scott Hahn (April 2004). 129

Reading Scripture as a Catholic Christian
  Interview with Scott Hahn (August 2008). 157

The Real Population Crisis
 Interview with Steven Mosher (June 2005). 187

The Conversion of Dietrich von Hildebrand
 Interview with Alice von Hildebrand
 (October 2000) 219

Guideposts for The Journey Home

Introduction
by Marcus Grodi

The following is a small sampling of the great variety of *The Journey Home* programs broadcast on EWTN, beginning in September 1997 and continuing by grace into the present, now with my son, Jon Marc, as the host. This selection features some familiar names, including the woman whose idea sparked this program. Mother Angelica hoped that the stories of conversion would encourage conversion, hope, and renewal in the lives of any who just might be flipping through the channels looking for some reason to just keep on keeping on.

Today the news, both near and around the globe, seems to be getting grimmer and grimmer. It's easy to see how anyone, without a firm foundation in Jesus Christ and His Church, might become discouraged, even to the point of despair. But the guests in this collection, each in their own way, witness to how God in His mercy reached out to them — even when they were as lost as lost could be — how He opened their minds and hearts, to let them know that He was always there, next to them, calling them home.

These episodes are not your usual *The Journey Home* episodes. They are mostly what we called "Open Line First

Mondays" programs, in which we invited a previous guest to return to spend more time answering live questions from the home audience, by phone or email. As a result, you get to hear more than just a short version of their conversion stories; you get to hear them answer a wide variety of questions, some of which may just be the very questions you yourself have on your mind right now.

I hope that these stories are an encouragement to you. It was one of the greatest privileges of my life to be able to host this program for twenty-five years—to meet so many inspiring Christian brothers and sisters, to get to know the fine staff at EWTN, and particularly to become at least a distant friend of Mother Angelica, God rest her soul.

If you have any questions after reading these stories, please do not hesitate to contact either EWTN or the staff at the Coming Home Network (www.chnetwork.org). It is our united goal to help you grow closer to Jesus Christ and His Church.

Sincerely,
Marcus Grodi

Our Continual Conversion
Interview with Fr. Benedict Groeschel, C.F.R.
(August 2007)

Marcus: Welcome to *The Journey Home* program. Tonight I have a special guest—Fr. Benedict Groeschel, C.F.R.. He's with the Franciscan Friars of the Renewal.

Fr. Benedict, it's great to have you here. Finally!

Fr. Benedict: Finally. It took me a long time to make *The Journey Home*.

Marcus: I know! You were the first person I ever saw on EWTN. Back when I was a Presbyterian pastor, I flipped through the channels and hit this Catholic network. I had no interest in watching it, but I saw this monk. And in Presbyterianism, you aren't used to seeing monks, and there you were with your gray habit and your beard, and I almost listened out of humor—"What's this monk going to say?" And then I found out, wait a second, what is he doing preaching the gospel? I wasn't expecting it, and I've been a fan of yours ever since then. I know that our viewers have been touched by your programs and your books, and I know they've been touched by your witness, but my bet is that they didn't expect that I was going to have you on my program to talk about your own conversion.

Fr. Benedict: Well, listen, let me tell you, I'm working on it. When people say to me, "Hello, Father, pray for me," I say, "Well, pray for me for my conversion." And they start laughing. Why are they laughing? I'm working on my conversion.

Marcus: Talk about your spiritual journey.

Fr. Benedict: It is interesting. I knew that I was going to be a priest when I was seven years old. I remember the day and the hour, and it had to do with someone whose name unfortunately has become associated with attacks on the Church and even pornography, and that's Walt Disney. In those days, Walt Disney's movies, when Walt was alive—he was a good man, a good Catholic—his films were moral films. The good guys did good, and the bad guys did bad. And I went to see *Snow White and the Seven Dwarfs* on the first run with my dad, and you remember there's a wicked witch; she's very convincing. And very hideous. I was scared to death.

Now, my second-grade teacher was a wonderful nun, Sr. Teresa Maria, the soul of kindness. And every day after school, she would leave the convent and go down to a nearby poor street, Westside Street, and she'd go into a tenement. She always had a box or a tray, out of which came steam on a cold day. So, I went there; it was a barber shop on the first floor, and in those days, all barbers were Italian. This was Giuseppe's. And I can still see myself getting up into the chair, that little chair the kids sit on, and saying, "What does the sister do who comes here every day?" And Giuseppe said, "She's a-take care of an old lady." I said, "Why?" "She's a-very sick." I said, "Where does she live?" "On top a-floor." So, I went around the back, and I went up the fire escape. And I got to the top floor, pulled over the milk box, got up, and there was the witch right there looking at me, three inches away!

I jumped off the milk box, ran down the fire escape, and ran up the street into the church to the altar of the Blessed Mother. I can see the blue candles flickering, and I'm praying there, and I said, "I wonder why the witch doesn't kill Sr. Teresa? Maybe it's because she's kind to her. And if people were kinder to witches, maybe they wouldn't be so bad." And something said, "Be a priest." Be a priest. It wasn't an audible voice. I said, "I don't wanna be a priest, I wanna be a fireman." "No, you gotta be a priest."

And I went out, and I looked at the priest's house, which was a bit foreboding-looking, thinking: "I gotta live in that house." I never said a word. But in the third grade, my next sister, Sr. Consolata, gave me a holy card, and she wrote on the back: "*Ora pro me.* Sr. Consolata." My father said, "Why did she write it in Latin: pray for me?" I said, "I don't know." He said, "Ask her." And she said, "Because you're going to be a priest." And I've never thought all those years of being anything else.

And when I was thirteen years old, I read the beautiful poem by Longfellow called "The Legend Beautiful," about a monk who's having a vision of Christ in his cell. And while he's praying, the bell rings to feed the poor, and he doesn't know what to do. Should he go? Or should he stay? Should he slight this celestial visit for a crowd of ragged bestial beggars at the convent gate? And so, he gets up, and he leaves the vision, works for hours with the poor, comes back, and the vision is standing there. And Christ says to him, "If you had stayed, I must have fled." And that made up my mind that I would be a monk or a friar of an order that worked with the poor. And that's what I did when I was seventeen. I joined the Capuchins, and I joined at a marvelous time. In the novitiate monastery at that time was a venerable servant of God, Fr. Solanus, and I served Mass for him many times. So, I got to know some saints.

Marcus: Talk, if you would, about the second conversion. I know a lot of Catholics watch the show, and they're inspired by converts, but they sometimes wonder whether they've ever had a conversion themselves.

Fr. Benedict: Well, I think all Christians need a second conversion. Sometimes I've heard some Evangelical Christians say, "I've been converted. That's it. I've been saved." No. We all need to be converted constantly. And that message is in the Gospel. No place does Christ ever say, "Sit back on your laurels; you've been saved; you've been converted." He is constantly calling the apostles, like Peter and the others. St. Paul never says, "I'm there, I don't have to …" No, he says "I press on, lest I, having preached to others, should be lost myself" (see 1 Cor. 9:27).

So, the second conversion is after a person has given up all deliberate sin, serious and even "small" sin, if you can use that expression. They're working to get over the egotism, the selfishness, the pride, the ambition, the self-importance, the resentments, the unkindness that we all have, and I don't know whether the second conversion ever gets finished. I'm a disciple, not only of St. Paul, but of St. Augustine, and he thought we stayed at it to the end of our lives.

Marcus: There's a verse I'd like you to reflect on. It's not an easy verse, but I think it seems to express what many Catholics might feel, and not just Catholics, but those who've lost children and siblings from the Faith. It's Hebrews 6:4–6: "For it is impossible to restore again to repentance those who have once been enlightened, who have tasted the heavenly gift, and have become partakers of the Holy Spirit, and have tasted the goodness of the word of God and the powers of the age to come, if they then commit apostasy, since they crucify the Son of God on their own account and hold him up to contempt."

Fr. Benedict: Well, the way he describes that person, that's not simply a convert. That's not simply someone who has accepted Christ. He is describing someone who has been at it very seriously for a long period of time, that has made real progress. There're a lot of people who would consider themselves good Christians, who don't quite fit that beautiful example in the Letter to the Hebrews. I tried to take this up in a new book I'm writing on the spiritual life. The last stage of the spiritual journey is called the "unitive way," and it fits that description. And I wonder if someone in the unitive way … I mean, it would be incredible to think that a person living in union with God would quit.

The people that I know who got lost along the way were never anywhere near that; they were struggling as we all do, with mediocrity. Look at St. Peter and the other apostles. They denied Christ, but they came back. There are lots of examples. Eleven of the apostles, or at least ten of them, are examples of people who were close to Christ, who knew Him in the most intimate way, who failed Him—"I don't know who you're talking about" (see Luke 22:60)—and yet they came back. So, I wouldn't give up praying for anyone. St. Teresa of Ávila, the great mystic, used to shock people by telling them that she prayed for the salvation of Judas Iscariot. "How could you pray for Judas Iscariot? He betrayed Christ!" And St. Teresa, who had been a worldly nun, said, "So did I, and I hope that I will be saved."

So, I think we should never give up on anybody, and there are interesting examples in Church history. There's a Carmelite monk who was condemned to be imprisoned in the underground dungeons for practicing black magic. Can you imagine? Talk about apostasy. And this man was down there in that dungeon, and he returned to God. He was excommunicated, but he returned to God. And crowds of people used to go down to talk to him and see him, and finally the word got out, and they freed him, but he wouldn't come up. He said, "I found God in this cell," and he stayed there and continued his preaching from there. That's the most extreme case I know of.

Marcus: You've written many books on conversion, and I have one in my room here, *Healing the Original Wound.* It's a wonderful book on the process of conversion. You also have *Spiritual Passages,* which is more of a psychological perspective on that. Given your understanding of conversion, let's say you're talking to non-Catholics out there, helping them understand the Catholic perspective of the journey of faith, of salvation. What would you say to them? How would you help them understand the Catholic view of salvation?

Fr. Benedict: Well, I'd say, first of all, conversion is a moral thing. You have to convert your heart to God, and a great many very good non-Catholic Christians are converted to God; they're deeply and sincerely believers. Tomorrow, I'm going to be speaking at a Southern Baptist seminary, and I'm sure I will be talking to many very real disciples of Christ.

The conversion into the Catholic Church from another Christian denomination is also an intellectual conversion. It's learning things about the very early Church and recognizing that the early Church is the Church that is the Catholic Church today. That's more of an intellectual thing. You take Cardinal Newman. He was a saintly man already. He was a very good Christian as an Anglican. And I think that probably for many people, probably yourself, the door to come into full communion with the Church of Christ has been to realize that many of the things said about the Catholic Faith are distortions. They're untruth. Scott Hahn speaks about that. He had read a book, *Roman Catholicism*, but when he finally studied, it was a different thing. There're a lot of misconceptions.

And then secondly, to understand the early Church, the very early Fathers of the Church, St. Ignatius of Antioch for example, who was appointed bishop by St. Peter himself. I mean, you're going back to the time of the apostles. And I heard a distinguished Protestant theologian, Robert McAfee Brown, say many years ago that the more that we look at the early Church, the more the signs point to Rome.

What's the great obstacle? It's the bad example of Catholics. Catholics have not done a good job of being the true Church. Look at St. Francis de Sales, the bishop of Geneva, Switzerland—although that was during the Reformation, so he was never actually allowed into Geneva. He was a very holy man, and his book *Introduction to the Devout Life* was read by Protestants everywhere, even though he was a Catholic bishop. And when Francis de Sales died, the Protestant people said that if all the Catholics were like Francis de Sales, there wouldn't be any Protestants. Protestantism represents a failure of *Catholics*, but not a failure of Catholicism. None of us would be anything but hopeless agnostics or atheists without the grace of God. None of us.

Catherine of Siena, Doctor of the Church, died when she was thirty-two years old. A lay *woman*, a reformer, an apostle, a *lay*person. And the popes were living under the French kings in Avignon in France. And Catherine of Siena wrote two of them letters to get back to Rome. But if they did, they'd probably die. So, when Catherine showed up at Avignon, the pope was happy to see her, and she came in, she made the proper courtesies, and she said, "Your Holiness, you stink." And he said, "Young woman, how do you know I stink? You came here from four hundred miles away." She said, "I could smell you in Italy." And you know what? Two days later, he left for Rome. He wasn't gonna mess around. So, like everything else, the human side of the Catholic Church constantly needs reform, and our three great popes of this time, John XXIII, John Paul II, and Pope Benedict, all are calling incessantly for the reform of the Catholic Church.

Marcus: John XXIII has a book of his own, *Journey of a Soul*, where he goes through his long struggles himself.

Fr. Benedict: It's about a second conversion.

Marcus: And it led to his own call for renewal.

One of the areas of confusion between Protestants and Catholics is the place of works in our walk of faith. Talk about that, if you will.

Fr. Benedict: I think *that* one is a somewhat phony argument; I think it's a semantic argument. When St. Paul is writing about works, he's writing about the mitzvah of the Jewish observance. Mitzvah is a work of the Law. If you grew up in a Catholic/Jewish neighborhood like I did, you hung around on certain days of the year because if they asked you to do something, you'd get a nice tip, because that was the day that Orthodox Jews had to do a mitzvah. A good work. And these works were called for by the Law—the observance of the dietary laws, the prayers, and things like that—and it was the belief of the people that these bought your salvation. And indeed, they were signs of faith in the God of Abraham, Isaac, and Jacob. But they didn't *earn* salvation. So, St. Paul was militating against that.

But St. James is the great antidote to all of this: "Show me your faith apart from your works, and I by my work will show you my faith" (James 2:18). Jesus tells us, "I was hungry and you gave me food.... I was hungry and you gave me *no* food" (Matt. 25:35, 42), with very different conclusions. So, *living* faith is what is necessary. And what the reformers were protesting about was a superstition existing in the very weak Catholicism of that time, weakened by the Black Death, which was the equivalent of an atomic war. It took one-third of the population of Europe, half of the clergy; two-thirds of the monks and nuns were wiped out—the monks and nuns died in such great numbers because they cared for the dying—and it was in two years, one-third of the people from Turkey to Iceland died. That was the fourteenth century.

Marcus: It's also probably fair to say that the priests who died were often the best ones. They were the ones that were helping.

Fr. Benedict: The Franciscans of the province of Paris, founded by St. Bonaventure, were wiped out to the last man. Every friar was dead. Probably out of thousands. So, it was a terrible calamity, and the Middle Ages was falling apart. And people who were unprepared and perhaps unworthy at times were in the clergy. There was a lot of superstition and a lot of simony. And the Catholics agreed. St. Catherine of Genoa, a laywoman, started the Reformation in 1490.

Marcus: Talk about her.

Fr. Benedict: St. Catherine of Genoa, a laywoman, ran the largest hospital in the world for poor people. She deeply affected the Augustinian Order, and the Augustinian Order had a branch like the order I belong to of the Franciscans, a reform branch. And one of the members of that reform branch was Martin Luther. They were working for the reform of the Church. People think that Luther got the idea first, but it came from Catherine of Genoa many years before. And in my book on St. Catherine of Genoa, I point out that she not only deeply affected both Luther and Calvin, but she was the ideal of the American holiness movement in this country in the nineteenth century: "Holiness unto the Lord." They published four biographies of St. Catherine of Genoa before the Catholics did. They didn't call her Catherine of Genoa, they called her Madame Adorno, which was her lay name.

Marcus: We have some emails ready for you, Father. Let's see what questions they're going to pose for you. Here's one. We've got a lot actually ready. This comes from Savannah, Georgia: "Dear Marcus and Father, my husband and I are trying to evangelize more to our non-Catholic friends and want to make sure we are using the appropriate version of the Bible, to have the best information and verses. What Catholic-edition Bible do you recommend, especially for evangelizing?"

Fr. Benedict: I would think the best one to evangelize, meaning to bring the good news, is the Bible a Protestant will accept, and that's the Revised Standard Version in the Catholic edition. That's neutral ground. And the Catholic edition has the seven apocryphal or deuterocanonical books, and I'd use that.

Marcus: All right, another email. This comes from Georgia: "Marcus and Fr. Benedict, I've always wondered why, when Jesus was on the Cross, He said, 'Let this cup pass from Me.' And, 'My God, My God, why have You forsaken Me?' Jesus obviously knew why He was sent to earth, so why does He say words that seem as if He wants His purpose changed?"

Fr. Benedict: Well, He actually said, "Let this cup pass by," at the Agony in the Garden. And the Church used those statements in a very important decision in the very early ages. Almost all Evangelical Protestants accept the teachings of the first six ecumenical councils on Christ. That's what the councils were about—the Trinity, the Incarnation, the virgin birth. Evangelical Protestants and the Protestant Reformers never touched the first six councils.

Marcus: I would say that they kind of ignored the Marian parts of those councils.

Fr. Benedict: Not originally. The Reformers never would have denied that Mary was Mother of God. Never. Because they would have ended up as heretics, which they didn't want to do. So, the sixth council in Constantinople proclaimed that Christ had two wills: a divine will and a human will. The people who denied it were called Monothelites. These two wills could not contradict each other, but they could be in contrast. So, during His Agony, Christ prayed, "Not my will, but thine, be done" (Luke 22:42). This is the human side of Christ speaking. And on the Cross, "Why hast thou forsaken me?" (Matt. 27:46). That is in fact a quotation from the twenty-first Psalm—that's the way the Psalm begins. So, Our Lord Jesus Christ was truly a man, He experienced things truly as a man and truly as God. Do you understand that? No, you don't understand that, nobody understands that. It's completely impossible to understand.

Marcus: Well, you point out a problem that's existed throughout the history of the Church, and that is that often we find truths that are difficult to put together, and maybe a characterization of it is that often, as Catholics, we seem to be much more comfortable with the both/and, whereas our Protestant brothers and sisters get caught up in either/or.

Fr. Benedict: Yes, it has been said that to be a Catholic, you've got to be able to chew gum and walk at the same time. You have to live with one God in three Persons, with one Christ and two natures, with human freedom and Original Sin. We have a lot of things like that, and those things are called mysteries and the mysteries of faith. A mystery, according to Albert Einstein—who loved religious mystery, particularly loved the Eucharist, loved to talk about the Eucharist — so according to Einstein, "A mystery is a reality whose existence we can perceive but whose inner workings are beyond our comprehension." And he said, "A person who does not look at the world with a sense of awe and wonder might as well be dead." That's Einstein. So, mystery is there, and religious mystery is extremely important. Otherwise, we are pretending to understand God, the depth of the riches of the wisdom and knowledge of God. As Scripture says: "How unsearchable are his judgments and how unsearchable his ways! For who has known the mind of the Lord?" (Rom. 11:33–34).

Marcus: And sadly, many of those battles, especially during the Reformation, were about trying to define aspects of the mystery that are really beyond us.

Fr. Benedict: Yes, the sad one was the Eucharist. The Church comes from the Eucharist. When Christ says to the apostles, "Do this in memory of Me," that's the beginning of the Church. Pope Benedict has pointed this out beautifully in his most recent letter, *The Sacrament of Love.* That's the difference between the Catholic and Orthodox notions of the Church, which are very, very similar, and the Protestant notion of the Church. The Protestant church is a collection of people who truly and honestly believe that Christ has become their personal Savior. They come together to pray, to do good things, to do missionary work, and that's why it's better to call it a church community. Whereas Catholics and Orthodox mean what Christ founded long ago: "This is My Church."

Marcus: I've got lots of emails, but before I go to them, I've got a question for you about the monastic life. When I was a Protestant, I did not understand the place of monastic life in the Church and the importance of the monastic life, even the mystery of St. Thérèse being called the patron saint of missions.

Fr. Benedict: Well, part of it goes back to the very, very early Church. Already in the second century there were Christians going and living alone in the desert or in communities. The first monks, like St. Pachomius, were ex-GIs in the Roman army, the Roman legions of the second, third century, and they took Christ as their model. A life of poverty, chastity, and obedience. St. Benedict was the great monk of the West who really organized it. And the monks of the West kept civilization going for six or seven hundred years during what are called, somewhat mysteriously, the Dark Ages. Almost everybody here has profited in their life by many things that they owe to the monks, including the preservation of Scripture, because they were the only people who could write. And then the idea of total dedication. Next to Our Lord, the most popular Christian, among Christians and non-Christians, is St. Francis, who was a friar. Friars are monks who work in the midst of the world. They're not solitary or in the wilderness. So there are Dominican, Carmelite, and Franciscan friars, many different orders and branches and twigs. My community's a twig. And St. Francis put it very succinctly: the rule of life of this order is the observance of the holy gospel, so it gives you an opportunity to lead a life of total dedication.

I've been a friar almost sixty years, fifty-seven years, and I own nothing. I have no finances of my own. I've never paid taxes because I've never had an income. I'm untaxable and un-suable.

Marcus: There're probably a lot of people out there this week, wishing they were untaxable.

Fr. Benedict: Everything I have ever earned has gone to the gospel, and quite legally.

Marcus: Let's take this first call, from Texas. Hello, what's your question?

Caller: Hi, I was just wondering how Father feels like his prayer life has changed since his accident?

Fr. Benedict: Well, when I woke up in the hospital after three weeks, I couldn't move. This arm didn't move at all. I couldn't speak. I had a respirator. I couldn't eat or have a drop of water for nine weeks. I said, "At least I can pray." So, I started to say the Rosary, and I said fifteen Rosaries a day and the Divine Mercy Chaplet. It's something you can do, and it helped me focus my mind. I would say if there's anything that has happened that I noticed, it's that my prayer is more silent. In some ways, I feel like I actually sort of did die. I got a second start. They said I'd never live, and I lived. They said I'd never think, and I think. They said I'd never walk, and I walk. They said I'd never dance, but I never danced anyway—it didn't make any difference. And I have no fear of death. I've been there and back. I don't remember anything, but I have the feeling that whatever God wants me to do, I'll try to do.

When you get up in the morning and you feel the pain and you know you're going to be handicapped for the rest of the day, it's a little depressing. But I take a deep breath, and I say, "Well, let's do what we can do." And I would say, I could not wish now that the accident had not happened, because many graces came from it, and so many wonderful people of all religions and denominations sent me emails of their prayers, including three Jehovah's Witnesses, Mormons, Buddhists, Hindus, everybody. I'm terribly grateful to them, and I pray for all the people every day who prayed for me.

Marcus: I know you could always speak of it, but especially now you can really speak of that old theology of "offering it up," right?

Fr. Benedict: Offer it up. What else was there to do? That's something the good nuns taught us all when we were kids. When things are going badly, offer it up.

Marcus: The great theology of redemptive suffering.

Let's take this email. It looks like somebody from your backyard, in the Bronx: "Fr. Benedict and Marcus, what advice would you give to a man who is homosexual and is having difficulty with celibacy? Is there a saint he can turn to for inspiration and help?"

Fr. Benedict: Well, this is a very interesting question. Cardinal Cooke, the saintly archbishop of New York, asked me thirty years ago to try to get an organization going for Catholics with homosexual orientation trying to lead a chaste life. I was too busy, so I asked Fr. John Harvey, who's been on EWTN, a wonderful, wonderful priest. He's now eighty-six years old, dragging himself all over the world with Courage. That's a wonderful organization. It's in the phone directory in New York, and it's in many cities, with plenty of very, very fine Catholic people who are homosexually oriented while leading a chaste life. And there are a number of Evangelical Protestant organizations, part of an umbrella group called Exodus. I think that people do better when they stay together and support each other. Now, is there a saint who struggled with homosexual ideas and attractions? We don't know, but I would feel certain that there is.

Now, there's something I have to say that's important. *Homosexuality* was invented at the end of the nineteenth century as a *thing*, as homosexual people say. It was never seen that way before. It was seen as a set of *tendencies*, as an orientation that was off, but not as a substantial thing. Now, Freud, who was an atheist and a materialist, and others of his time, saw it as if it were this *thing*. And I don't agree with him at all. If a person says to me, "I'm a homosexual," I always say, "Oh, I thought you were a person." I thought you were a person. Let's start with that; God made persons. It's a cross. It's a difficulty. Anyone who struggles with this deserves our encouragement. If they fail, well, people fail in other ways. Heterosexuals fail all over the place. Look at the media. Sin is by no means confined to the gay scene, and unfortunately in this country and this corrupt culture, anti-culture, people are seen only as sexual objects.

Marcus: Would you say, then, that one of the key problems here—not just with this particular view of homosexuality as well as aberrant heterosexuality—is a poor formation of conscience?

Fr. Benedict: Absolutely. Or no formation of conscience. Or an anti-formation of conscience, which I blame the media for. I see the greatest danger to the United States from the media, which comes together as a reptile—it's not even a wild beast—and with apologies to iguanas. The media entices young people. Media stations are directed at young people with constant sexual excitement and often homosexual orientation. And I want to tell you, folks, we just passed the last step down, because I am told that on the college campuses now, bisexuality is the big thing. The homosexuals are being left as Puritans in the background. People are having boyfriends and girlfriends at the same time. This means that they experience a terrible lack of identity. And this may solve the whole problem. You know why? Because it may bring this country to repentance. If somebody told me that in fifty years this country was very, very religious, very repentant, and very puritanical, I would not be surprised. Because remember the Wild West? It's the Bible Belt. All those guys out there with the saloons? There's a church on every corner in the Bible Belt where that Wild West was. So, we may be heading to a gigantic religious conversion.

Marcus: Here's one of my views of that. There're two great commandments: love the Lord your God with all your heart, mind, soul, and strength, and love your neighbor as yourself. And God would not call us to do something that we couldn't do by grace. We all have a desire within us to love God, but people who aren't formed rightly go off after other kinds of gods. We all have within us a desire to love one another—it's in there, men to men, women to women—but our consciences are so poorly formed that we don't understand that drive, and so we end up saying that this attraction is wrong as opposed to helping us understand what it really means.

Fr. Benedict: It's a distortion of reality. Masculine friendship, friendship between men, has been there since the beginning of the world, but it is distorted by this intrusion of libidinous sexuality into it. So, in the old days in psychology, if you had any friendships with people of the same sex, you were homosexual. It's insane! I have to say that we have a whole new psychology now, it's called positive psychology, or the psychology of virtue. It started at the University of Pennsylvania. Dr. Beck, Dr. Seligman, and others, they're saying that mental health comes from virtue and the practice of virtue. They identify virtues as core qualities that are identified by moral philosophers and religious figures as good, and their list is Plato, Aristotle, the Old Testament, the New Testament, Confucius, St. Augustine, and St. Thomas Aquinas. The University of Pennsylvania is doing better than a lot of Catholic universities.

Marcus: Let's take this email. It comes from New York: "Dear Fr. Benedict, I often wonder why some people have faith, and even among people of faith, there seem to be different levels of faith. Does Christ call people to different levels of faith and conversion, or is it a response from the person's heart? I would appreciate your insight as a psychologist and a priest."

Fr. Benedict: My guess is it's a bit of both. A person can receive a beautiful beginning of the gift of faith, the seeds, and yet they may not care for them. As Christ says in the Parable of the Sower, some of the seeds fall among the briars and on the rock. Another person may not receive much of a gift of faith, but they may respond to it very well, and this is why we have hope for the salvation of those who are not Christians. "I have other sheep, that are not of this fold; I must bring them also.... So there shall be one flock, one shepherd" (John 10:16). And it says in John that when Our Lord speaks of being lifted up for the salvation of the world—"I, when I am lifted up from the earth, will draw all men to myself" (John 12:32)—that He said these words, indicating the kind of death He was to die in order to bring together the scattered children of God. So, I have great hope. Each person has to respond to the gift that they've been given, and I'm busy worrying about myself.

Marcus: We have another email here: "Father and Marcus, since God's will is done, what is the purpose of prayer? Can prayer really change the course of things?"

Fr. Benedict: Well, as we know from the parables, Our Lord is very clear that we should pray to change the course of things. The Parable of the Importunate Neighbor. Or the Parable of the Unjust Judge, with the widow who is driving him crazy. "Ask and you shall receive" (see Matt. 7:7). So, Our Lord tells us to ask. The divine will is utterly mysterious to us. When people say, "Okay, I accept the divine will," do you think they know what they're talking about? God has no past; he has no future. St. Augustine says to God, "Through Your today pass all tomorrows and become all yesterdays, but to You, neither tomorrow nor yesterday have any meaning, for all things simply are." So, you can get yourself entangled in great troubles like positive predestination and things like that, trying to understand how we have some freedom but God knows all things. It's better sometimes to leave it alone, because human pride will lead us to try to understand God.

Marcus: What are your words of encouragement to very sincere people who want to do the will of God but can't seem to figure it out for their own life?

Fr. Benedict: We all find ourselves in that position. And I say: stop, pray, and listen. People don't listen when they pray. It says in Scripture, "Be still, and know that I am God" (Ps. 46:10). Stop and pray. And we're afraid to do that because we're afraid we might hear something we don't want to hear. And if it seems suddenly that we ought to do something that we don't want to do, that very well may be the will of God. Twenty years ago, I was praying about the situation in religious life, and I was very, very displeased by the skepticism, worldliness, worldly attitudes that had crept in, because I knew saints in religious life, I knew Fr. Solanus. And suddenly it seemed that we would just leave our beloved order and start a reform movement. It was the last thing in the world I ever wanted to do, and that made me suspicious that it might be what we were supposed to do. I had no assurance it was the right thing. I thought maybe we'll fail. And I knew what I would do. I couldn't go back. I would ask to be a priest in the Deep South and ask for an African-American parish because I get along perfectly with African-American people. I'd be too happy.

But it did work. We have 130 members. The average age is thirty-two, and if I drop dead, it'll get down to twenty-nine. It was supposed to be; it had to be God's will, because *we* couldn't do it. The other day, at the profession of our young brothers, I said to Fr. Andrew, who's the other old man, "You know, it's a work of God. We could not have done it."

Marcus: You wrote a wonderful book, *The Reform of Renewal*. It's ten, fifteen years later now?

Fr. Benedict: Twenty years later. I'm coming out with a new book shortly, called *Reform Now*, because I think we have missed the boat very badly. But the JPII generation, the young people from eighteen to thirty-five—not all of them, but a representative group, and you see them in the other denominations as well—they're clamoring for something to get them out of the cesspool that American culture has fallen into.

Marcus: Let's take this email from New York: "Dear Fr. G. and Marcus, was Judas predestined to betray Jesus? And if the answer is no, then if he didn't betray Him, how would the Easter message have turned out?"

Fr. Benedict: Again, you're into that mysterious area of the divine will, and there are places where it sounds like he was predestined, and there are places where it sounds like he was free. Surely, he had some freedom, and he certainly, even after he betrayed, had the freedom to repent. But the Church has never said that he is lost. The Church has canonized thousands of people and said that they were saints, but they've never "canonized" a sinner and said he was in Hell.

Marcus: Let's take our next email: "Good evening, I truly enjoy your show, Marcus—heartfelt thanks for your work. Fr. Benedict, can you talk a moment about what your recommendations are for someone who is looking for spiritual direction? Where and how should one begin?"

Fr. Benedict: Well, years ago, when there were lots of priests, there were lots of spiritual directors around; occasionally religious sisters or even laypeople are trained as spiritual directors, that's not as unusual as you think. But people need training, and there aren't very many places to train people. We have one in New York for spiritual development, but that's rare. And so, I think most people realistically have to get group spiritual direction from reading and from what we're doing right now. All my books are meant to be spiritual direction. I don't write any book that's not meant to be spiritual direction. I never give a talk or program that's not meant to be spiritual direction to help somebody else on their journey to God. I have no interest in doing other things, and you can get a lot of spiritual direction by just listening.

Marcus: All of your books that I've read, I've really appreciated. The little synopsis of Augustine, *Augustine: Major Writings*, is a wonderful, good book. There's also the book I mentioned earlier in the program, *Healing the Original Wound*, a wonderful synopsis of the journey that takes you from sin and helps you understand the place of Christ's redemption. It's a wonderful book which I'd recommend to any of you who are following our program.

So, we'll get one more email in quickly. This comes from Arizona: "I asked my devout mother why she is not Catholic. She said it's because so much of Catholicism (dress, ritual, and pomp) looks pharisaical. How does one respond to this? Especially when the contrast between the poverty of Jesus, St. Francis, and the historic wealth of the Church is so difficult to reconcile?"

Fr. Benedict: First of all, you ought to talk about the historic *poverty* of the Church ... you know, almost all the Catholic property in Europe was confiscated in the nineteenth century. You see the great cathedrals? They don't belong to the

Catholic Church. Notre Dame in Paris? It doesn't belong to the Catholic Church; it belongs to the French government. Actually, Trinity Church in New York, which is an Episcopal church, has a property value that exceeds the value of the Vatican. Because it's Wall Street. It used to be the parish fields. That's what I'm told about Trinity Church.

Now, the Catholics used to go in for pomp, I'm sorry to say, and I have seen it become a heck of a lot less pompous since my years as an altar boy. And I think if you watch the pope on television, he is the servant of the servants of God; this elderly man looking for a quiet retirement of writing books is there, and he's totally and absolutely given to his apostolate.

Marcus: Father, before we close, can we have your blessing?

Fr. Benedict: O Lord, in Your goodness and mercy, bless us all. Bless everyone listening and their families and friends, especially those who have weak faith or no faith. Send Your Holy Spirit upon us. In the name of the Father and of the Son and of the Holy Spirit. Amen. God bless.

The Stages of the Spiritual Life
Interview with Mother Angelica
(August 2000)

Marcus: Welcome to *The Journey Home*. As I contemplated beginning this series of *The Journey Home*, I thought back to the beginning and remembered the first time that I sat down with the person whose idea it was to start the series: Mother Angelica herself. I remember sitting down with her as she described why she had envisioned this particular kind of program, and it came from what she had received from our viewers—from your letters, phone calls, and emails, talking about your own struggles with the spiritual life, your own frustration sometimes with children and friends who've left the Catholic Church, and sometimes losing hope with their own spiritual journeys.

So, as I thought about who would be the perfect guest for this first episode, to start our fourth season of the program, it only made sense that we invite the very person who thought of the program—Mother Angelica herself.

Mother Angelica: Wow, I'm excited. The Lord has always been so providential with us, you know? So, I'm ready for your questions.

Marcus: All right. Well, the audience probably wonders, "Was Mother a convert?" But there's a sense in which we all have to be converts, isn't that true?

Mother Angelica: I think we all have or should have—we probably do and don't realize it—conversion experiences. It's not dramatic like St. Paul; we don't even have a horse to fall off of. But I think all through our life, everybody's had a time, and it may be a short time, maybe just a moment, when somehow the thought of God and loving God and living like the Lord says in the Gospel makes more sense than in others. Now, we may not follow it, but we all have these conversion experiences that are so small sometimes we don't notice them.

Marcus: That's right. And as I reread your book—which I recommend to all those who haven't read it, *Mother Angelica: Her Life Story*, by Dan O'Neill—it reminded me that as we look at our lives, we can look back and see ways in which what we went through then makes sense now, and we see how almost everything now has been a continuation of all of that. But at the time, we didn't know that.

I don't know if the audience knows your early struggles with the spiritual life, and what I had proposed to you is to talk about your early journey, your spiritual faith. But if you could, relate it to the way the spiritual writers talk about that way in which we progress: from the beginnings of the purgative way, to a more illuminative way, to growing in union. Tell us about how the Lord brought you on that journey.

Mother Angelica: You know, the Lord uses ordinary things to do great things. When my mother and father were divorced when I was six years old, to me, it was a hair-raising experience. I was hiding behind an ice box, because my grandma and grandpa went to the court, and before they left, my grandpa said, "Now pray the judge lets us keep you." Well, I was petrified. So, all I could think of was hiding somewhere, so I hid behind the ice box. I wouldn't come out when they came home. They kept calling and calling, and I was just breathless, I wasn't going to move. And finally, he caught on, and he said, "The judge said we could keep you here." Well, I just shot out of there.

Now, that's an experience that I'm sure a lot of people have had. They don't see much in it, but there's a lot in it, because God has our whole life in His mind. I would not have the compassion I have today, I don't think, for those people who are divorced or alienated in whatever way, if I hadn't gone through that experience. But I didn't have God in that experience. But it's okay, because *God had me* in that experience, and it was a part of a puzzle that would lead me into religious life years later. But you've got to go through certain pains and certain problems, and they may not be great tragedies in your life. Disappointments. God uses a lot of disappointments, and things, and people, and as we go along, God uses those things to bring us closer to Him. That's what we don't understand.

Marcus: Some people will see those negative things in their life as, "Oh, what's going wrong," or, "What have I done wrong?" Whereas I noticed in your own story, at some point the grace of God started to get you to ask, "What are You saying to me, Lord?" To see in this—although it was a negative experience—to see that a still, small voice was there.

One of the things you realized that was an awakening for you was that because of your parents' divorce, you were viewed a certain way by other people.

Mother Angelica: Oh, yeah, definitely.

Marcus: And that fed your ability to have compassion later.

Mother Angelica: Right. I was ostracized because I was the only child of divorced parents. I didn't have a place to invite other people, so that cut out girlfriends. Now, that aloneness has been a great help to me. Today, we have no silence anywhere. Even if you're in an elevator, you think you'd have some quiet, but now they've got on some kind of music or something. So, our minds and hearts are filled with noise. It doesn't necessarily have to be music—just plain noise.

And I think I began to learn. God was working on me. That took me time to understand. God was working on me where "I was a loner"; I was forced by society to be a loner. And to me, if I had people around, that just made more trouble. At recess, I would go out and sit on the steps somewhere, and they were playing with a rope and wearing themselves out, and I thought, "How dumb. How stupid." So, even at recess, I stayed by myself.

Marcus: I remember you had one experience with your teacher saying you could do so much more if you tried. And your anger.

Mother Angelica: Oh, yeah. She had a whole lesson on this one person, and when I left the classroom, she called me back, and she said, "You know I was speaking about you. You could be all these things," that she expected me to be. And I looked at her, and she said, "What are you going to do about it?" I said, "Nothing. I don't like you, and I don't like people." I was gone, and I'm sure she was happy I was gone. But what seemed useless and fruitless in those times, God was preparing my heart, to listen to Him. See, I didn't want anybody else, because I knew, with divorced parents, it wasn't going to pay anyway. I wouldn't get friends anyway.

So, God, in His infinite mercy, was at work. You just spoke about the three ways of spirituality—purgative, illuminative, and unitive. God was working on the purgative right off the bat. But I didn't know that. And in that purgative way, we don't understand a lot of things. We rebel against what's happening, or worse, we just don't care what's happening. So, all of these things, as I look back, were absolutely necessary for me, to have something inside burned away—the desire for the world, desire for things, desire for anything—all this was eliminated slowly by circumstances. Those circumstances, as unfair or unjust as they were, God used them to put me aside in solitude. That's the purgative way, for the average working person, for the housewife or whatever. There's that element of purification that the spiritual writers call "purgative" because it's detaching us from what we think we want. And that's in every layperson's life. God has arranged for all of us to be holy.

Marcus: And that's one of the reasons we're talking about this. These spiritual challenges are not just for religious; they're for every single one of us.

Mother Angelica: We rebel against them because we're always looking at human justice. "This isn't right; that isn't right; this isn't right." But as I look back, God was preparing me to go it alone. But I had to wait until I was eighteen to pass from purgative to the light.

Marcus: We'd better define *purgative*. There are probably people that don't know what purgative means.

Mother Angelica: *Purgative* means our purification. We started being purified very early in life, and I did very early in life by that divorce at six. Hell begin on that day, and I knew it. Even at six years old, I couldn't have defined it, but I knew that something terrible happened, and I was going to have to go through it.

But I never thought of God. I never thought, "Oh, God, help me here." I never did. But even in this pain and sorrow and disappointment and poverty and hunger, God was working, because I began to learn very early in life that none of these things really mattered because I could be happy without them.

Marcus: So, the purgative way is God teaching you the importance of detachment.

Mother Angelica: It's a way of detachment. Riches and poverty aren't what make you detached. I've found some very wealthy people who are totally detached from their wealth, from everything, and we can find very poor people who spend their whole time wishing they had something else.

So, the purgative way, which everybody goes through, is a purification, a detachment from the things that really don't matter.

Marcus: So, what was it that the Lord then used to pull you from that first stage of the journey?

Mother Angelica: It was my first healing. I had a stomach obstruction, and I couldn't eat. I was down to crackers and tea and very little things. It was a couple of years like that. And I was nervous; I didn't sleep at night. It was a mess. And a woman said to my mother on the bus one day, "Why don't you take her to see Mrs. Wise?" She was a stigmatist who had been healed herself and was a very holy woman. I didn't know what stigmata meant, and my mother wanted to take me although there was a blizzard! I thought, "Well, who cares? It's not going to mean anything anyway." I didn't have faith. I was not healed by faith; I was healed by God's mercy. God must have said, "If we don't do something with this creature, it's going to be a terrible thing."

Anyway, I went to this very poor house; the woman was poor, but she was holy. And for the first time, I saw something I never saw before; this person had something I hadn't seen before. There was no halo or light, but there was something there, and I was amazed. But being the pagan that I was, I shook that one off and went home, and I said this little prayer to St. Thérèse, the Little Flower. And the ninth day was a Sunday. And I got up, and I knew I was healed. I had a terrible pain in my stomach, and I went to the kitchen, and I said to my grandmother, "I'd like fried eggs." She said, "You can't eat fried eggs." I said, "Yes, Grandma, I've been healed." But you don't tell that to an Italian grandmother, I can tell you that. Because she just stood there with her fork in her hand, and she said, "What?" I said, "I've been healed, Grandma. Can I have fried eggs?" She said, "Sure." And I said, "Perhaps some bacon?" "Bacon?" I said, "Yeah, bacon." "Okay." And I said, "Grandma, I would like a cup of coffee."

She was amazed. She was just standing there with her mouth open. My mother woke up by that time, and she was hysterical: "What do you mean you're healed?" And she said, "Where are you going?" "I'm going to Mass." See, that was the first time I knew I had to do something godlike. I had to do something that was on His side. She said, "You can't walk all that way." I said, "Yeah, I can." I got dressed, and I walked three miles. Now, you're talking about somebody who could hardly keep her knees together, and that was the first time in my life that I knew God knew me, loved me, and cared. And that was a surprise to me. But see, it took all of that pain, suffering, and aloneness to teach me, and then this miracle to me was awesome. I went to Mass as often as I could, and I made Stations of the Cross every day.

Marcus: So, whatever happened to you spiritually at that moment changed your heart, all of a sudden, to have a hunger and a thirst you didn't have before. I would like to talk about that, if you would, because not everybody has these miracles, and we all have a two-by-four between the eyes. So, talk about, maybe in a more general way, what is this second conversion, and how can we identify it in our own lives?

Mother Angelica: Well, we all have it. We just don't see it. Say there's been a tragedy in your life, a disappointment. There was something wonderful ahead, and it didn't happen. Instead a tragedy hit. Now, we don't call that an ecstasy, we don't call that a conversion, but it's an opening for a conversion. Why is it an opening? Because I have two ways to go. I can go to the world, I can bury myself in the world, or I can turn to God. Everybody, I'm convinced, and I don't care if you're a dishwasher in a restaurant or a ditchdigger or an executive on top of a building, you do have *many* opportunities. If we would just turn to the Lord and say, "Lord, I'm desperate." Even if one falls into grave sin, there is something there that says, "Look, this is not all there is," number one, and, "You'd better seek the One Who can help you." All those are conversions.

Marcus: Like the spiritual writers I've been reading, which again, in becoming Catholic myself and reading Catholic spirituality, it's been such an awakening for me. But to hear the way you describe it, sometimes that conversion happens when God seems to draw Himself away from us.

Mother Angelica: Oh, yes, very much. He does everything possible to make us seek Him. See, that's what happened to me. The fact that I was healed, I feel, has to do with the mission God was going to give me way over here. Because in one of the ecstasies Mrs. Wise had, the Lord said to her, "Rita will do great things for the Church," and she was so surprised. And she said, "Rita? My Rita?" She was shocked. And the people around her told me years and years later she couldn't get over what He was saying. But you see, the Lord was preparing me just like He prepares everybody. It may be something as mundane — well, it's not mundane — as getting into this particular college you wanted to go to, and you've got your heart set on it, and you think you've got your schedule all ready, and your friends are going there, and all of a sudden you don't make it. Now you're saying, "Is that a point of conversion?" Yeah! Because there you're desperate, you're alone, you don't know where to go, and you don't know what to do. That's the formula for conversion. But you see, because we read too much, I think of the ecstatic books, we're waiting for this big thing to fall on our head, but it doesn't. It's the ordinary problems, the ordinary tragedies, the ordinary thing that hits my heart and makes me feel terribly disappointed or terribly lonely or terribly detached, especially when someone dies. That is the turning point to go to God.

Marcus: Isn't it true that sometimes it can be a blessing that we didn't have this big miraculous event, because we'd never get beyond that big, miraculous, powerful experience?

Mother Angelica: No question. And then you have to realize the purgative way means purified. Anything you purify—if I have a rusty pipe in my hand, and I want to make it beautiful again, I've got to take a file; I've got to get that rust off—from the purgative to the illuminative, a lot of rust has to go.

Marcus: Talk about the illuminative now, in your own life. What does *illuminative* mean?

Mother Angelica: In my life, I realized one day after making the Stations that I had to be a nun. I was the only one my mother had. I told my aunt, my uncle—they thought I was absolutely mental. But I pursued it. And none of the active orders—the orders that were teachers, nurses—would accept me because my grades were so low.

Marcus: So, that was a blessing in disguise.

Mother Angelica: It was, but I didn't know that. I was crushed. So, finally I went to the St. Joseph Sisters in Buffalo. And after three, four months, they wrote and said they'd decided to take me. The counselors had hesitated because they felt that I had a contemplative vocation. I didn't even know what that meant. So, I went to Msgr. Habig, all excited that I was accepted, and I said, "They waited so long because they thought I had a contemplative vocation." And he said, "Yes, you do." I wondered, "Why didn't you tell me this a long time ago, you know, I've been looking and looking?" I said, "I do?" He said, "Yes, you do. And I know exactly where you should go." I said, "Where?" He said, "Cleveland, Ohio. St. Paul's Shrine. The Poor Clare Nuns. That's where you have to go." Wow. And that was another turning point because I didn't know anything about a contemplative order, let alone that one.

I didn't know what it meant, but I knew I had to go. I ran away from home. I had to wait two years because I was too young. I had to wait until I was twenty-one. I said goodbye to my mother on August 15, without her knowing I wasn't coming back, and my boss gave me the fare for a bus. I went to Cleveland, and that was another turning point. Because I had to step into something I knew absolutely nothing about. And then I began to see what I could never before have seen—why it was.

Marcus: Would you say that this second conversion opened your heart to be much more willing to say yes to God—though there's a lot of unknowns—to be willing to take bold steps in areas of trust that you never would have before? Would that be a way of describing it, as a part of understanding our second conversion: this openness to God?

Mother Angelica: Yes. There are three things that go hand in hand: the purgative, the illuminative, and the transforming. The first, I was *resigned* to God's will: I had a vocation. But when I went to Cleveland, I was *conformed* to God's will: I was accomplishing it. Now, being conformed to God's will and going into the illuminative way are basically the same. Because in conformity, I understand a little better, I *will do* God's will. But it's still a mystery. It isn't that my will and His will are one will.

That's where the average layperson can make giant steps, because he also has that darkness in his life; he also wants to do God's will. That's resignation, that's the purgative way—you just know you've got to change, you know that.

Marcus: It's a mystery of both/and. It's what God's doing, and our obedience.

Mother Angelica: That's right. Obedience becomes clearer as we go to that next step. In the purgative way, I'm obedient—but I've got to change. I'm impatient—I like everything done yesterday; I don't like to wait for anything. I have a temper—and this has got to go. So it's kind of a rise and fall, you're going up and down. Now, as you pass to the illuminative way, you're going to *do* that one thing that's going to change your life.

And laypeople do the same. You may have lost a job, which you loved—they go out of business, and now what? But all of a sudden, something else comes up that maybe you've never done. And you say, "What's that got to do with holiness?" *Everything.* Because now you're going into the darkness of something new that you're not sure of. So now, you're going to grow in faith, you're going to grow in hope, and you've got to grow in love. You don't do anything for someone unless you love him a lot. So, now, even the average layperson who is in the world and working in the world suddenly becomes not of the world. See, there's that giant step. So, now they begin to want to read a little bit more because their heart is hungry.

They already see this is a good thing, it's a wonderful thing. They've made that little step into ice water, and now they're ready to see God and to love Him in the very thing they've had to give up. Now we pass from something that was purgative—something hard to do and I am not too sure—to the illuminative. Now, I'm sure. It's still hard, but there is a greater hunger for God when we take that next step.

Marcus: I remember the moment when I became more aware that I had made that progress, as I looked back and recognized that something had changed in my heart. When something great would happen in my life, I remember when I used to say, "Wow, I was good." But now all of a sudden, my heart was saying, "Thank You, Lord."

Mother Angelica: Thank You, Lord. Exactly.

Marcus: That change, that's grace. When our minds are changed to seeing Jesus first as opposed to ourselves. Now, the other thing that the spiritual writers talk about is that when we move from the purgative to the illuminative, a lot of those early sins that are more obvious are gone, but new ones start popping up.

Mother Angelica: That's right. Because you see yourself more.

Marcus: Talk about that old struggle. A person in the illuminative life, they're not perfect yet, right, Mother?

Mother Angelica: Right. You see, there're a lot of things about ourselves we don't know. We couldn't take it if we did.

Before, I'm struggling with marbles. Now, I've got to move mountains. And the Lord said if I had the faith, I could move this mountain. The mountain is me. Over here, in the purgative way, I could attest to my actions—not too good. But over here, in the illuminative way, I know my *thoughts* are not too good. My motivation is not right yet, because now you begin to compare your motives with His, to compare your ideas of justice with His ideas of justice. And you cannot read the Gospel without knowing right off the bat He doesn't think like you think. He thinks differently. There's a man that had ten talents, another with five, and another with one. He takes the talent away from the guy with one and gives it to one who has ten. And the apostles were amazed. They said, "Master, he already had ten. Why didn't You divide it with the guy who had five?" You see, we don't think like He thinks, and this is a surprise.

So, I'm forgetting the marbles now. I know those are no good. And now I've got something bigger. And there's where we're talking about conformity. In the illuminative way, I must become conformed to God's will.

In the purgative way, I'm thinking about it, and I resign myself: "Eh, it's kind of a rotten deal, but I'll do it." In the illuminative way, it doesn't seem that way, because you *know*, because you're beginning to feel in your heart—you've gone from your mind now to your heart—and you're beginning to say, "I don't want to hurt Him. I need to do this for Jesus." So, all of a sudden, Jesus becomes a dominant factor in your motivations, in your ideals, in what you want, and that happens to everybody. People like me that He had to hit on the head and make suffer, and then at that point, you begin to realize the beauty and the power of suffering. Before, it was in the way, unfair, unjust, and you can dump it. No, no, no.

Suddenly, I began to think, "This is good, this is good for me." Then you begin to look back and say, "Well, you know, my father left my mother when I was six. And that was good for me, because it gave me something I would have never had." But I only see it in the illuminative way. I couldn't see it before.

Marcus: It's good in the sense of Romans 8:28. "In everything God works for good."

Mother Angelica: And they taught me a lot.

Marcus: He's shaping you.

I'm going to pull you to the third stage. Since those years, so much has happened. The Lord has brought you here to Alabama, the monastery, all that's happened here. Now, you would never have dreamed back in those early days that you'd be able to take the gospel all around the world. What about that third stage? With all that's been happening, what about the unitive movement with God? How has that been in your own spiritual journey? I would think that the distractions of everything would maybe even be a barrier to that spiritual walk with Christ.

Mother Angelica: Yeah, it could be if you don't give credit where credit is due: to the Lord. At that point, you can never say, "Gosh, I did a good job." You can't because you know in your mind, in your heart, you may have said yes, but after that, *He* bears the fruit. And you know that. Why do you know it? Because you still got a memory with A and B in it; you've got the little marbles rolling around inside of you, and you've got the big mountains you've moved or tried to move.

All that settles in the back of your mind somewhere and keeps the lid on the ego. At that point, you can never say, "I did a good job." The only thing you can say is: "He did it all." I have to say that because I know myself, and probably, hopefully, as I grow older, will know myself more. In the unitive way, we give all the credit to Him because we've finally found out that's where it belongs. You say, "Mother, you did a great work on this," and I'll say, "Yeah, the Lord really blessed us. He's done great things." You say, "Oh, you're being humble." No, I'm not. It's the first time in my life I'm being truthful about what He does. You can't take any credit for anything because you're so aware of yourself.

You see, the world tells you, "No, you're great, you're this, you're that," but see, the Lord in the Gospels says, "Unless you *empty* yourself." Success could be the worst thing that ever happened to somebody. Because if you're not struggling to be united to Jesus, you can't take success. It's not a good thing sometimes; sometimes it's a terrible thing. I've seen many, many people elevated to great positions, and they were so much better when they were fussing with marbles. Something can happen to you on the heights; there's spiritual pride. Not pride meaning I've got a better car than you have, but spiritual pride that says, "Well, look what I did." But you see, as you're getting closer to that unitive way, the only thing that matters is Jesus.

In the unitive stage, even though maybe you don't understand God's will, why He wants this, you do it quickly, because it doesn't matter anymore whether you like it or don't like it. What matters is only that He wills it. You see the difference? Now we've got to that point—"Lord, whatever You want, I want. I don't want any other thing." So, that brings my needs down quite a bit. See, what makes us lose peace is that we want so many things. All their lives, some people, they've wanted this, and then they wanted that. But what you notice is that, as people get older—too bad it takes old age—they need less. And it's not because they're rickety-rackety, it's because in their hearts they know that real peace and real happiness and real joy come from that union between you and God. And if you're lonely, it's okay. You've lost everybody, well, you miss them—but that's okay, you're on your way there. If things don't go your way, you'll make do. There's not that struggle to do what I want to do. It's the greatest peace we can have.

Marcus: That's the freedom of the unitive way.

Let's take our first caller. A young woman from Anchorage. Hello, what's your question for us?

Caller: Hello, Mother Angelica. It's so awesome to see you on *The Journey Home*. My question is: What's the first step for a young woman who loves God but doesn't know how to tell if that feeling might be the beginning of a vocation? Should she go talk to a priest? What if she's not getting any encouragement from anybody she knows? What should she do?

Mother Angelica: Well, I think a vocation is a call. It isn't something you choose from twenty other things you could do. It's a call. And we need to find out, is it a call to holiness we have or is it a call to complete dedication? And many confuse the call to holiness with the call to a religious vocation. That's the first thing you have to discern. Are you married? Well, then if you're married and have children, you're called to holiness but not to a religious vocation. But if you're free and you're of age, the age that they accept religious vocations, then if you have it in your heart, I would begin to look. It's very simple. You have to find out: Do I want to be a contemplative? Do I want to be in an active order? Do I want to take care of children and the elderly? Then I would look for that particular way of life, and there are religious orders of every way of life you can think of. Then I would visit, and all this time praying.

If you go from place to place to place, and you don't really find it, then I would take it that God wants you to live a single life, a consecrated life perhaps, or just a single life of someone who knows God and loves God. And then you can arrange your day between your work, your family, your extended family, your neighborhood family, and how you can help them. You're going to Mass, looking at your life, and doing things for others. You can arrange your life in such a way that it's really religious, though you're in the world. Like St. Catherine of Siena; she wore a third-order habit, but she was not a religious as we consider today.

Marcus: Wasn't Rose of Lima the same?

Mother Angelica: Rose of Lima was the same. So, in that way, you've got to find out what God is calling you to, but we also have to understand that God calls many, many people—all people, everybody—to some kind of dedication to Him because you were created by God, for God, and to be with God forever. But we all do it in a different way.

Marcus: And the beauty of what I've discovered in the Catholic perspective is that it isn't just me and Jesus and what God would be calling me to do. We're being sent as a part of the Church. Our gifts are for the good of the Kingdom, the good of the Body.

Mother Angelica: There's where the Mystical Body comes in, because whatever I do, if I am called, affects the whole Body.

Marcus: Let's take our first email: "You talked about being resigned and then being conformed to God's will. Does the ability to be conformed come from grace, or is it an act of the will? And if it's an act of the will, how can I learn to control my will in unity with Christ?"

Mother Angelica: The desire to be conformed is a grace from God. He inspires you to come higher in a different realm. But your will has to say yes. Your will has to accomplish what you just said yes to. And even though we may fail every so often and kind of bounce back to resignation, that's okay. Come up and say, "Lord, You know I love You," like Peter (see John 21:15). "You know all things, Lord. You know I love You, and I want to do Your will, and only Your will." Now, the more we do that little exercise—it's like anything, we have to *exercise* our will—we exercise our desire to be holy. It comes to a point where conformity is easy, easier; conformity is almost immediate from exercise. It's a combination of His grace and your yes. They have to go together.

Marcus: And you know, this is one of the beauties of Catholic theology, because a large segment of our separated brethren believes in the complete depravity of the will, an inability, such that we do not have freedom of the will, we do not have freedom to respond, which then, when you take that equation, leaves everything up to God—you're either predestined or you're not, you're elected or not. And in essence, it even throws the evil back on God. Like, what if I didn't have the grace? What if I didn't get the grace? Well, was that my fault or God's?

Mother Angelica: God gave us free will. The reason it's free is that I can say yes or no to God. But that doesn't mean I can do as I please when I please how I please. It means that He's giving me an opportunity and giving Himself the joy of you loving Him so much that you're more than willing to do something you really don't want to do.

Marcus: Let's take our next caller. This is from Louisville. Hello, what's your question?

Caller: Yes, Mother Angelica, you've had such an interesting journey, and I was wondering what do you think is the most amazing thing that God has ever asked of you?

Mother Angelica: Oh, that's a big one. I think the most amazing thing was leaving my mother, for the simple reason that she was always heartbroken. She cried every day. When I was a kid and went to school, I was always afraid. She was very suicidal. But when I had the courage to say, "Goodbye, Mom," she didn't realize what I meant. Because she went to the right to go to her office, and I went the other way, every morning. That was very difficult for me, and I was amazed at the grace. I've been amazed at all the wonderful things God has done for His people out of a tiny inspiration. It's scary to me. None of these were great big things that happened that made me say, "Oh, isn't that wonderful?" Sometimes, it was as simple as a phone call I made that changed the entire aspect of this whole network. I could have said no to it because it didn't make sense. That amazes me.

When the Child Jesus said to me, "Build Me a temple"—I didn't even know what a temple was—"and I will help those who help you." And I didn't want to tell anybody. But it began. I'm like a kid in a big field—a baseball field or football field—and I watch Him working. To me, that's absolutely amazing. The Lord has asked us to build many things and do many things. If I want to look at the greatest thing He's done, I think it's the Temple.[1] All the other things we've done are communications, and they feed the mind, and they feed the heart, but the Temple seems to be different. It reaches into the soul. It happens every day, it reaches down into the soul until people feel, "There's something wrong in my life." Awesome! And these kinds of people can jump from nowhere up to unity. That's an awesome thing to me. I see people who haven't been to Confession for years, haven't done a thing for God for years, haven't even wanted to do anything for God, and suddenly they walk into that Temple, and they see themselves in a whole new way. Some of them just fall flat on the floor, and their lives have so totally changed, it's just amazing!

So, we've done everything to teach, to bring the Faith back, to bring people back to the Lord and back to Church. But the Temple is something different. I'm not too sure yet what it will do, but it's different.

Marcus: I think, if we look at the things that the Lord has been able to do with you, it should help us look at our lives and see what the Lord could do through us if we were willing to say yes.

Mother Angelica: Yes, you have to say yes.

---

[1] The Shrine of the Most Blessed Sacrament near the sisters' monastery in Hanceville.

Marcus: Lord, whatever You want to do, wherever You have me, what can You do through me here?

Let's take our next email. This is from Columbia, South Carolina: "You spoke of union with the Lord. What if I fear that union? He may ask something of me I'm not yet prepared to accept."

Mother Angelica: I think that's a temptation, and I think we do an injustice to God. Because He's not there to grab something from you. He's there to ask you, you see, and if you say no, He'll do something else with you and wait till you're ready. He's a loving God, a compassionate God. But I would strongly suggest that if you're sure God is asking you for *anything*, do it. But the only thing He really asks is a total conversion, and that has to happen almost every day. I have to get up in the morning and say, "Lord, I wasn't too patient yesterday. I really messed things up. I want the grace today to be like You." All of a sudden, I'm starting the day then with an act of humility—I know I goofed. Secondly, I know I can do it again today. But thirdly, I know Who can help me. I also know that if I say yes to Him in the smallest thing, He's going to flood me with grace. God gives a lot more than we can give. And He never asks anything for our harm. You know that beautiful poem of Francis Thompson? He said to Francis, "What I took from thee, I took not for your harm, but only that you would seek it in My arms." And if you could remember that, if the person who's asking you the question could remember that one thing: whatever He asks is never for your harm.

Marcus: Mother, I'm going to ask you a question about how we can pray for you. I'm one that believes that every one of us needs to read the book of Job and put ourselves in the story as if God and the devil were talking, and God says, "Well, look at My servant Mark," and the devil says, "Well, You give him to me, and I'll challenge him."

Are the struggles there for you, in your spiritual journey? Is there something that we can pray for, for you and the sisters?

Mother Angelica: Oh, yeah. Because first of all, as you get older, it isn't that you're not sure you did the right thing, but always some kind of temptation is there: Did you do it really for Jesus? I have my own soul I have to look after, because as St. Paul says, "What does it profit if I save the whole world and lose my own soul?" (see 1 Cor. 9:27; cf. Mark 8:36). So, I need prayers for myself.

And I need prayers for my sisters, who consistently pray before the Blessed Sacrament for everybody in the world. Sometimes, because of this massive communication media that the Lord has given us, we hear of people who have been converted. But there's that constant giving, giving, giving, and we cannot want to know, we can't desire to know the fruits, and that's the problem of contemplative life. A layperson can go out and educate someone or teach someone, and they *see* that person blossom. That is not true, or not so much, in contemplative life. So, my sisters need prayers, that they persevere in the darkness of faith, that they persevere in hope, that they persevere in love, because they have Jesus, and they have learned that they have to be satisfied with God alone.

And we need prayers for the network. We need prayers that it will continue to grow and continue to draw people back to Jesus—that's exciting!

Marcus: Mother, we have one minute. Could you give a parting word of encouragement, if maybe there is someone out there that would like to grow closer to Christ?

Mother Angelica: Yes. It's very easy to go closer to Jesus. Tell Him very often during the day, "Jesus, I love You." We all want to hear that. And He wants to hear it too. "Jesus, make me holy." And then during the day when things are hard or easy or good, say "Thank You, Jesus." If somebody gives you a piece of cherry pie, say, "Oh, thank You, Jesus!" If you get a corn on your big toe, "Thank You, Jesus." Little things. Don't try to do big things. The little things like that all day long make you holy faster than anything.

Marcus: Mother, thank you so much for joining us on *The Journey Home*. What a wonderful pleasure!

Obstacles to Coming Home
Interview with Mother Angelica
(September 2001)

Marcus: Welcome to *The Journey Home*. I remember back four years ago when Mother Angelica suggested the program and shared the reasons why she felt that this program was a necessary part—one of the pieces of the puzzle—of what she wants to accomplish with EWTN. And to be honest with you, I was humbled when I was asked to be the host, and I wasn't sure I would last a month or two, and here we are starting the fifth season.

It's the great grace of God speaking through the testimonies of men and women who, through their love for Jesus Christ, have been opened, either to come into the Catholic Church for the first time or to come home to the Church that maybe they left early in their life and then discovered the great beauties of it through God's grace. It's very appropriate on this fourth anniversary of the program then that I invite the foundress and inspiration, not only of EWTN, but of *The Journey Home* program, Mother Angelica herself.

Mother, thank you very much for joining me on *The Journey Home.*

Mother Angelica: Oh, my pleasure, my pleasure. I've always wanted such a program from day one.

Marcus: Well, it really has been a great success, and I'm humbled by that, because I always remind the people that it is the guests that make *The Journey Home* program—their love for Jesus and the Church.

Mother Angelica: And the guests see some things that Catholics maybe have lost, and that Protestants wonder about, you know, "Why do you believe this?"

Marcus: And I know from our emails and letters that we have a large number of non-Catholics that watch this program. So, when the guests and I prepare for the program, we're not just talking to the choir here, we're talking to others that we want to become a part of the choir.

So, the last time you were on *The Journey Home*, you inspired us all by describing the three ways of the spiritual life in relationship to your own journey. And I thought, "Well, what do we talk about this time?" And what I'd like to do is to pose some "devil's advocate" questions that non-Catholics pose and that stand in the way of them coming into the fullness of the Church, and then have you reflect on those, if you would, and maybe from your own spiritual journey share how you dealt with those issues yourself.

To me, one of the biggest—which, to me, seems absurd—misunderstandings that Protestants and non-Catholics have about Catholics is they might say, "Catholics aren't even Christians. They don't even believe in Jesus." Talk about the reality. In your old introduction in the program, how did you always end it?

Mother Angelica: "Tonight, we're gonna talk about Jesus!" I think this misunderstanding, it's because of the sacraments we have. You see, the sacraments have Jesus, or rather, give Jesus to us in a very special way. The Bible is the Word of God. But so is the Eucharist—the incarnate Word: Body, Blood, Soul, and Divinity.

So, we're concentrating on Jesus among us in the Church, in every church. But we're reminded that "if you keep the commandments, we will make our home in you" (see John 14:21–23). That's Jesus. That's the Father, the Son, and the Holy Spirit. So, what we Catholics don't do most of the time is just say, "Jesus saves," meaning He saved *me*. You see, in order to be saved, we feel you need to go to Confession. So, these sacraments seem to take the place of always talking about Jesus, where in fact, they give you a union with God that's not possible otherwise. If I've committed some grave sin, I can say to God, "I'm sorry," but I will never *hear*—you know, we sin with our senses—but I will never hear, "I absolve you." Who absolves? A man? I wouldn't tell a man anything. But this is God. So, instead of talking about Jesus, if the Catholic is true to their Faith, they feel they're talking *to* Jesus. Not just about Jesus, but *to* Jesus. That's a difference that I think is very wide.

We get to the point where religion—and that can be in the Catholic Church too—religion becomes a matter of rules. Most Catholics and Christians would make better Jews. They're more Old Testament. They don't realize it. For example, if I feel that God is going to make me wealthy, healthy, and wise because *I* did something—you give Me a hundred dollars and I promise you're going to get a thousand—that's a recompense. God doesn't owe any of us. So, we have to be very careful that we don't mix invoking of the name of Jesus with the reality of *receiving* Jesus. And that's why there seems to be, in the Catholic Church, a lack of Jesus.

Marcus: One thing I've noticed. I was brought up Lutheran, which is very parallel to the Catholic Church in many ways, and it seems to me that on the one hand you have the beauty of the sacraments and the liturgy. But by the same token, there can be a great danger, when we become so routine, so ritualistic, that we can lose Jesus in the midst of that. For example, every priest in the world must say the Daily Office, but you can say the Daily Office and never actually pray.

Mother Angelica: And some don't say it. That's the worst.

Marcus: But you can just say it by rote and never connect with the heart. I think that's why people outside, they look at Catholics and maybe see us doing these things and wonder: "I want to see if you have a relationship with Jesus in that." And we have to remind Catholics that that is what it's all about.

Mother Angelica: The problem with the Catholics is they haven't been taught. It sounds like a criticism; I guess it is. I'm noted for that. They haven't been taught the spiritual life, haven't been taught to *apply* the sacraments to their life. I can *believe* that Jesus is in the Eucharist; I can believe in the Immaculate Conception; I can believe that Baptism takes away Original Sin. But if it doesn't affect my life by a deep spirituality ...

Marcus: Otherwise, it's up on a shelf.

Mother Angelica: That can happen with sacraments, that can happen with all the beauty in the Church, and it all happens because the average person is not taught even one of the multitude of kinds of spiritualities. For example, I'm Franciscan, and my particular thrust is that I love Jesus: Do you love Jesus? Why don't you love Jesus? Now, if I were Dominican, my approach would be that faith is an intellectual assent to truth—Thomas Aquinas, wonderful. And if I belonged to a teaching order, like the sisters of Mother Cabrini, I would be working in great earnest for souls: Who can I help? Who can I talk to about Jesus? What can I do?

Marcus: You touch on an interesting thing for me, because when I became Catholic, I envisioned that I was entering this monolithic united body, and I'd come through this gate and there it would be. And then what I found is this amazing, but at times troubling, diversity. And actually, all these spiritualities can be paralyzing. To which one do I go? And I actually think that what you've just said helps your audience understand the beauty of EWTN, because it's keyed in on your spirituality. That's why we focus on Jesus.

Mother Angelica: Well, in every spirituality, there is the Cross, because we believe that, without it, we cannot exist in this life and be purified so we can meet God face to face—you're talking about an awesome Being, an infinite Being, Who reduced Himself to be a man, while never losing His identity as God. Well, we're not willing to lose ourselves. St. Paul said it nicely; he said, "Empty yourself." "Die to yourself," Jesus says. Okay, we're not wanting to do that. Instead, Catholics can be accustomed to think: "I went to Mass, I went to Communion, and I go to Confession once a month.

Finished. That's all there is to it." Well, all that is very exceedingly beneficial, but it's not all. Because I have to remember my weaknesses so that I *don't* sin. I have to *love* my neighbor, and the new commandment—to love one another as He loved us—is much harder than the old one. If I have to love you the way I love myself, it's very finite.

Marcus: The spiritual writers remind us that our daily walk involves a guarding of the heart.

Mother Angelica: A guarding of the heart. And an acceptance of the cross of the present moment. Humility—that's the lost virtue. Like fear of the Lord. Who fears the Lord today? That's why they say there is no sin. Well, I've got news for you, buddy, because St. John says, "If we say we have not sinned, we make him a liar" (1 John 1:10). Wow. Somebody ought to read that from the pulpit.

Marcus: You were touching on one of my favorite subjects. This absence of the fear of God is something we need to wake up to, especially as parents bringing up our children in the way of the Lord. Yes, it's love, but it isn't just all lovey-dovey. What makes love *real* is fear of the Lord.

Mother Angelica: I had a group of women here, this was in the '70s, and I had a few Catholics—and the reason I knew they were Catholic was they couldn't find the Scripture I was talking about. And I said, "Do you know that the Father, Son, and Holy Spirit dwell in you?" Neither Catholic nor Protestant knew it. Neither one. They said, "What?" I said, "They live in you, in me, all of you." I mean, they were shocked. "You mean God lives in me?" So, I brought out all the Scripture, Baptism, and the rest. See, that kind of spirituality is absolutely necessary, along with truth. Otherwise, there's nothing there.

Marcus: In fact, I've often thought about that when I see people debating over intellectual truth. Is it faith alone, not works? Or no, is it faith and works? And they fight. And I think, unless you have a converted heart, you're both wrong.

Mother Angelica: That's right.

Marcus: So yes, Catholics love Jesus. Those that take the time to study the Faith realize that it's really an absurdity to think that Catholics aren't Christian.

But maybe some think that because there are some bad Catholics around. And in the history of the Church there *have* been some bad popes, bad bishops, bad cardinals, bad laity. And so people take that as a reason to write off the Church. All right, as Catholics, how do we deal with this?

Mother Angelica: Well, if our dear Lord had Judas, we can expect some bad Catholics and bad Protestants and bad ministers and bad priests. Why? Somewhere along the line, they forgot Jesus. They forgot our obligation to be like Jesus. I'm not supposed to be like a politician. I'm not supposed to be like some famous man. I'm not supposed to be like anyone except Jesus. But our ambitions are in the wrong direction. And I think the reason for that is that we live in the world. But we don't have to *become* the world. Our Lord said, Father, "I do not pray that thou shouldst take them out of the world.... They are not of the world, even as I am not of the world" (John 17:15–16).

Because we all have free will, there will always be some bad people. You even get bad popes. But I am to pray for them. I am not to criticize them. We're not all the Immaculate Conception—neither Protestant, Catholic, Buddhist, nor Mohammedan. They are all in the flesh; they have all been given by God a certain personality, a certain talent by which they can become like Jesus. And I don't care who they are or what position they have, if they don't aim for that, they're not gonna make it.

Marcus: The spiritual writer that I was reading recently, Fr. Lallemant, talks about this issue. He points out that there are two things that often stand in the way of people moving in the grace that they have. First, there is pride, and he says it should drive us to great humility. I mean, if someone given that much grace can fall—what about us? But secondly, he says it shows you how devastating venial sins are to the spiritual life. People can get focused on, "Well, I haven't done this mortal sin," but be blind to the effect of the little venial sins. Let's talk about that, mortal sin and venial sin—maybe for the Catholic who thinks, "Well, I haven't done any mortal sins this month, I don't need Confession"—and the blindness of that.

Mother Angelica: Well, the blindness is we don't understand Confession. We think, "If I don't have mortal sins, I'm okay." Here's a cup. It's empty. If I attempt Chinese torture and let a drop fall into it time after time, it's going to be full. Mortal sin is one smack—*boom*—full. Adultery, stealing, fraud, slander—all these things can be mortal sins. If you ruin a man's reputation, and he's finished. Stealing, embezzling. Lying to the point where you ruin somebody's reputation. So, a mortal sin totally tears God away from you. If you break the Commandments, for example. A venial sin, it's little bit by little bit. Now what happens is I become indifferent after a period of time. I run the danger of becoming lukewarm because I'm in the habit of not really caring. And I'm not talking about scrupulosity. Scrupulosity is stupid. God is greater than you are and greater than your sins. But venial sin becomes indifference after a while. Then worse, like you just said, "I don't commit any mortal sins." Well, maybe not, but I have venial sins aiming for it. I'm going to become lukewarm. And what did Jesus say about that? "I wish you were hot or cold" (see Rev. 3:15). Cold—you can handle somebody cold. But lukewarm—He said, "I will spew you out of my mouth" (Rev. 3:16). That's just not a nice saying. It's nauseous to even think about it.

When we get to that point where we don't feel we need to go to Confession anymore ... You see, the Catholic does not believe once saved, always saved. Everybody knows you cannot just do as you please. You can't say, "I love You Jesus," and give Him a fist in the face. Even on the natural level, we call that abuse, physical abuse. We verbally abuse God by saying, "I will not serve." Now, what's the difference if I say, "I will not serve," and try to kill you, or if I say, "I will not serve," and give you a dirty look? Well, there's a lot of difference in the gravity of offense. But if I pile up the lesser offenses, you see? And you can't just say, "It's only venial sin." Because it piles up. You can't. I think to every non-Catholic, every non-Christian, that makes sense.

Marcus: When you look at the lives of popes who didn't live up to their Faith, well, in a way that's a witness to what venial sin can do in a person's life. Little by little by little by little. The coldness, the lukewarmness, the indifference.

Mother Angelica: The problem, I think, with many of the popes—they were appointed by *family prestige*. But there's one thing that happened. Even though they were snuck in by politics, one thing always happened, which to me proves that the Catholic Church is the right Church: they never erred in doctrine. And they could be pretty bad.

Marcus: Some of them were close to erring, but the Spirit stopped them, prevented them.

Mother Angelica: The Spirit always inspired them to speak the truth when it came to doctrine. Politics, they were in too hot. But that also proves to me there is no church in the world that would have lasted without our sacramental system, with all the beauty of the spiritual life and all the saints, through all of this. You know, Napoleon went to the pope, threatened him, and said, "I can destroy the Church." And the pope said, "If we haven't done it, you're not going to do it." See, that proves to me that the Spirit is in charge of the Catholic Church. And even though there were times we had one pope, two popes, three popes all at the same time with all those shenanigans—still, we always knew and obeyed the right pope. So, I think we have to remember all that.

Marcus: And a reminder, "There but for the grace of God go I" (see 1 Cor. 15:10).

A third area that stands in the way of people misunderstanding Catholics is: Why do you worship Mary? Why do you pray to Mary rather than Jesus?

Mother Angelica: Well, the misunderstanding is in the beginning of the question. We *don't* worship Mary. You can only worship God, and Our Lady herself can only worship God.

Our Lord Himself says in the Commandments you have to honor your mother and your father. When we speak of God the Father, designing that His eternal Word would become man, He had to create someone special, especially beautiful and holy, not only without sin at conception. Because we don't understand how it happened, we say it didn't happen. But that's a lack of humility on our part: you can't know and understand God. So, when you say that, you're accusing God of not following His own Commandments. He honored His Mother.

Of course, they always bring up the Wedding at Cana, and that always burns me up. "What's it to you and to Me?" Well, He asked her to say "fiat" to His coming. We don't think of what might have happened if she said no. So, her fiat brought Him, and it was her fiat that had to begin His three years of miracles and ministry. That's why He said to her, "What is it to you and Me?" (see John 2:4). In other words, you're going to start My Passion, you're going to begin now. You know what you're doing? You're going to begin My public ministry. You brought Me here, and now you are going to begin. "So, what is it?" He wasn't correcting her. He was reminding her. "What is it?" And she turned around, she knew immediately, and she responded as always: "Do whatever he tells you" (John 2:5).

And that's why we have to love Our Lady. She suffered. Any mother who is a real mother has to know that, to see her Son in that condition and then *stand*. She *stood* at the foot of the Cross, and I have to be *grateful* to this awesome woman. Not only was she conceived without sin, but she became the Mother of the Most High Word of God. The Father would have to make her very special for our sake. Everybody thinks she's taking us away from God—oh, goodness, *no*! She said, "Fiat." She said, "Do whatever He tells you." And she *stood*. And that word *stood* is not just another word indicating a position. It indicates her own position as Mother of God, which means she, too, added her pain, her terrible pain, with her Son. And St. Paul says that. Every good Protestant knows what he said: "This is a wicked generation, and your lives should redeem it" (see Eph. 5:16). Are we going to say that His Mother didn't redeem it along with us? That's why I don't understand any reason that people have for not loving Our Lady. And the awesome thing is that Jesus said, "Behold, your mother" (John 19:27). How do you explain that? "Oh, it was just John; he's gonna keep her in his house."

Marcus: Well, that's exactly the way we explained it. I'm wondering if maybe another part of the difficulty is when those on the outside of the Church watch Catholics and they don't understand. So, let's say a non-Catholic is watching a religious praying the rosary beads before a statue of Mary. The outsider says, "That looks like idolatry to me." It's because they just don't understand it.

Mother Angelica: They don't understand that it's Scripture. The Rosary is the life of Jesus, how Mary looked at it, how Mary absorbed it, how Mary lived it. She lived the Cross. We run as fast as possible away from it.

This morning, I had a terrible headache. What did I do? I offered it up to Jesus. I said, "Jesus, I give You my headache." But I went straight for two Tylenols. And that's fine, that's what God wants you to do. Now, if it doesn't go away, you bear it. But Mary, she bore the same pain as Jesus. No mother can say the same. Now, the Maccabees' mother, she also had to watch, and no one will say she didn't love her children. And when the last son was about to die, she said, "Now, don't you give in."

So, I don't understand why we object to God's gift to us as Intercessor. She is the Great Intercessor. If our dear Lord can hardly refuse her anything, well, I wanna go to that person. I've had people come to me and ask for prayers; they do it all the time. They ask you for prayers, though both of us are poor sinners. I'd rather ask one from His Mother.

So, what people might think is worship is nothing but love. But I admit, there have been fanatics in the Church.

Marcus: They go a little extreme in another direction. That's why the Church has had to define what's true.

Mother Angelica: But that's why we can trust the Church, who tells us that we can go this far, and no further. And that's the beauty of the Church. If you don't have that authority, when and how do you ever know?

Marcus: Mother, we talked a little bit about the fear of God. Did you want to comment a little bit more about that? I mean, there's a problem today.

Mother Angelica: It's a big problem, and we're not too clear even about the two kinds of fear. There's servile fear. It's better than nothing, but it's not that good.

Marcus: It's the very beginning. It gets us to turn.

Mother Angelica: That kind of fear, though—servile fear—is only being good because you don't want to go to Hell. See, that's servile fear. Filial fear is the kind we want. That's one of the gifts of the Holy Spirit. The first gift of the Holy Spirit is fear of the Lord—filial fear. Since Jesus came, the reason I must not sin is because I don't want to hurt the Father.

Say there's a cookie jar here, and a mother says to her son, "Now, don't you take a cookie, you're gonna spoil your appetite." He says, "Okay, Mom." And all of a sudden he's looking at that jar, and he's looking at that jar. Nope, he can't stand it, and he opens it, and oh no, now he smells it. He can't stand it. That's how we deal with temptation; we play with it. And he picks one up, puts it down, and then all of a sudden takes a chunk. Now he hears his mother—*bump, clank*—he's looking out the window. Fear. Fear, meaning, he's going to get it, he's going to be punished, he's going to have to go to his room, he's going to get spanked, and he doesn't want that. He didn't *not* take it because he loved his mother, but because he's afraid of the consequences. Now, that's better than eating the whole piece, but it's not good.

Okay, so now say he looks at that cookie jar, and he says, "You know, I'm really gonna hurt Mom; she's gonna be very disappointed in me, and I don't wanna hurt her." He walks away. It doesn't mean he wasn't tempted by the cookie. It doesn't mean he didn't think about it. His motive, though, for not taking it, see, we don't have that anymore. Nowadays it's just, "Do what you please as long as it's what you want to do." That's why so many young kids are living together, not being married. They think that's the right thing to do. That way, if you get tired of each other, you just walk away. As long as we have that attitude toward God, there is no love. Well, if there is no love in your heart, in other words, if you're not good because you don't want to offend God, out of love, then I can guarantee you're not only not growing in holiness, but you become habituated to sin until you kill your conscience. It's a serious thing.

Marcus: I was reading in the life of Fr. Louis Lallemant about the balance between the fear of God and the love of God. It seems that in the last fifty years, we've swung from one extreme to the other. It's almost as if, to take the cookie jar image, the mother would say to the child, "I don't want you to eat those cookies. In fact, some of those in there are poison. You do not want to touch those. But if you do, I love you anyway. I'll love you just the way you are." And so, there's no fear of punishment. The kid's going to eat all those cookies down in a minute, and that's what we've ended up with.

I want to read this quote. After they describe his whole life and all his commitment to holiness, the biographer says, "The fear of the Lord, which is the basis of all other gifts and the foundation of the whole spiritual edifice, was always in him, as it is in the true children of God."[2]

Mother Angelica: It comes to you from Baptism, from Confirmation.

Marcus: It's a reminder to us parents that this fear of the Lord has to be a part of catechesis.

[2] Frederick William Faber, ed., *The Life of Father Louis Lallemant, of the Company of Jesus*, in *The Spiritual Doctrine of Father Louis Lallemant, of the Company of Jesus*, trans. Peter Champion, 3–36 (London: Burns and Lambert, 1855), 6.

Mother Angelica: Let me just show you what happens if you don't have fear of the Lord or you don't want it. The fear of the Lord is the first gift of the seven gifts of the Holy Spirit. I have to have that fear in order to receive piety, the second gift, to love my neighbor. I love you because Jesus lives in you, the Trinity lives in you. I don't want to offend Him in you, and I don't want to offend you. But I have to know that He is *our* Father, not only my Father. But I can't do that without fear of the Lord. I don't want to offend Him in you, and what did Jesus say? Jesus said, "Whoever gives ... a cup of cold water" (Matt. 10:42)—and He said *cold*, and I think that's wonderful—gives it to whom? "To Me." So, if I'm going to love you, the fear of the Lord—meaning love for the Father—enables me to love the Son in you. And I'm not going to give you lukewarm water; I'm going to give you cold water.

The next is fortitude, the third gift of Spirit, because I've got to have perseverance in this whole thing. I can't be nice to you today and then hate you tomorrow and then be nice again the next day. I can't do that. I need strength to love you. I need strength to continue my journey, loving God, because of all the distractions of the day.

And the next gift is counsel. I need discernment. We don't have discernment anymore. You see how everything hinges on fear of the Lord? If I don't have fear of the Lord, I cannot discern whether this is a sin, whether it's a venial sin or a mortal sin—if we're going to be counting things. Am I offending God at this point in my life? Am I making the right decision? So, I have to discern three things. Is this the Holy Spirit inspiring me? Is it a human spirit, my own? Or the evil spirit? So, I have to have discernment. There is no discernment today, and that's why you see people doing strange things.

Marcus: Otherwise religious people doing strange things.

Mother Angelica: All is based on the fear of the Lord. Now, these are what we call the four "working gifts" from the Spirit, that I have to use day after day after day to arrive at purity of heart. But I also need something deeply spiritual, and the next gift is knowledge. I need to know the "one thing necessary." Our Lord spoke of that with poor Martha. And Mary chose the better part. I need to know my Scripture. What is Jesus like? How did He act in this situation? How does He want me to act in this situation? I need to know the Scriptures; I need to know the Word of God. In fearing the Father, I need to know the Word that He gave me. I need to be detached from sin, from greed, from ambition, from jealousy—and that's the gift of knowledge. I need to be detached.

Now, understanding comes along, and that's a gift from God that's unique for each one, for me personally. The first gifts are more general, and we all have to practice them. But this gift, as I begin to pray, I have to know who I'm praying to. I must strive for contemplation. I must begin, like Franciscans do, or are supposed to do, to see God in everything. A little flower, a mountain, rain, the power of the ocean. In my brother. In a baby. If we saw God in a baby, would we kill them?

And it all starts with the fear of the Lord.

Now, the last gift is the greatest of all. It kind of takes all these little jewels, and puts them together in a big, massive ring: the gift of wisdom. The gift of wisdom is not to make you appear smart. The gift of wisdom is to unite you to the whole Trinity in such a way that you have His thoughts—His will is supreme—that you're totally detached, that you can discern at an instant.

Our Lord did that so well because He *is* Wisdom. He said to Peter one time when he kind of blew off and said that, "Yeah, my Master pays taxes," and He came in and just said, "Peter, who pays the taxes? The king or the servants?" And he said, "The servants." Jesus said, "Well, just so you don't get embarrassed or scandalize them, go catch a fish. And in his mouth, you'll find two shekels. One for you and one for me" (see Matt. 17:24–27). You see the wisdom of Jesus that kept Peter from imprudence—and alive?

Marcus: And Scripture tells us at the beginning of wisdom is the fear of the Lord. It says that many times in Scripture.

Mother Angelica: You can't get away from these things, and if you don't live of the gifts here, we have that awesome, wonderful place called Purgatory.

Marcus: Well, there's another can of worms! We do have a caller waiting for us from Iowa. What's your question for us?

Caller: Oh, I'm so happy to talk to both Mother and Marcus, my two very favorite people. Thank you! Mother, the Ten Commandments really are not talked about any more in the sermons that we hear at Mass. Why is it? Is it due to Vatican II? Just what's going on here?

Mother Angelica: No, it wasn't Vatican II. This whole century started way, way back, started in the 1800s, 1700s. The idea grew and grew and grew that the only commandment was to love God, so you could do anything else. And Our Lord found fault with that. He said: "You say that you don't have to give to your parents, that you don't have to follow that commandment. You're going to give it to the temple treasury instead. You hypocrites" (see Mark 7:11–13). And I think the reason that we're not speaking of the Ten Commandments is—and it's contrary, totally contrary, to the Word of God in every way—that the average minister, priest, they don't want to hurt your feelings, they don't want you to walk out from Mass angry. You're sending them slowly to Hell, and you don't want them to be angry?

See, it's the job of a minister or priest to preach the truth. And the Word. If you don't speak the truth—and the Word is the Truth, He said He was—if you don't speak of *His* Word, there's nothing else but the lie. If you lie to make somebody feel good, you're not keeping even the first commandment. The first commandment is the basis of all the rest. You're going to go against every commandment if you don't love God, totally detached of everything and everyone. Detached—not indifferent. Detached, meaning that God takes your heart and soul and nothing else does.

Marcus: In a way, this always gets us back to what you were talking about, the fear of God, because as our Holy Father reminds us—what's his most common phrase? "Be not afraid." It doesn't mean: "Be not afraid of God." He means don't be afraid of anything else.

Mother Angelica: Because God is supreme.

Marcus: You should fear God. You shouldn't fear the people. You shouldn't fear for your reputation. You shouldn't fear that people may not love you.

Mother Angelica: That's why parents don't correct their children. They're more concerned about the children always loving *them* than if they're offending God. We don't want to preach the Ten Commandments today because we want to be popular: it's not the "in" thing today. The Gospel is two thousand years old; it's old-fashioned; it's not up with the times. All of this is a non-fear of God. Not even a servile fear. It's a non-fear. "I wanna please the people." If you're a politician, you want to go to the next step.

Marcus: But Mother, "God loves you just the way you are."

Mother Angelica: He loves me just the way I am. But He desires my conversion, otherwise, I can't live with Him forever. God loves me as if no one else existed—I'm not a group; I'm an individual that God takes care of and loves. I read one of these accounts of people who die and come back. This woman was the town gossiper, but she was a "good" woman. She was at church every week, and she was very popular, and she did all the work you can do, and she made all the parties. But she was the town gossiper, and she died. She said, "I saw the Lord. And He looked at me, and He said, 'Nothing but leaves. There's no fruit. Just leaves.'" So, what she *did* didn't matter a hoot, because she was tearing down everybody every day. She bore no fruit. He didn't even tell her where she was going. He sent her back. See, now here is the mercy of God with someone with just leaves. Here's the goodness of God and the grace of God, and He loved her to do that.

Marcus: Yeah, that was mercy because in John 15, He says, "If you don't have fruit, you're torn up like the branches and thrown into fire" (see John 15:6). That's our calling in life. What is our fruit?

Let's take our email. This is from San Francisco: "Dear Mother Angelica, for those of us who do not have the direct line to God that you do, how does one determine when to move ahead and when what seems to be a godly thing (nothing opposed to faith and morals) may in fact be of one's own wishes?"

Mother Angelica: Well, there again, we need the gift of counsel. Isn't that what we said? We need the gift of counsel, to know the difference between the Holy Spirit of God, the human spirit of man, and the enemy, the evil spirit. I would, first of all, pray for the gift of counsel, that's what I would pray for. Secondly, if you got an inspiration, *wait*. If it's of God, He will open the door. If it isn't, it'll just blow away.

Marcus: Well, there's another virtue that the enemy tried to destroy in the twentieth century, and that's the virtue of patience, waiting on the Lord, waiting for the Spirit to continue to inspire us. And we're not just individuals; we are part of a community that can help us discern whether that calling is of the Lord, and so there are spiritual directors.

Let's go to this other email from Houston, Texas: "Dear Marcus and Mother, I am a cradle Catholic who is in the process of rediscovering my Faith. I understand that it is necessary, in order to live my Faith, to pray in order to come to know God. But I find every time I set time aside to pray, something comes up, whether it be work related, a friend comes over, and so on. Praying seems to get pushed aside. Can you give me some advice on how to really give God the best of my day?"

Mother Angelica: When you get in that position of being too busy, you have to make the time at some point. Get up earlier in the morning before there's too much traffic, before you have to fight traffic. To pray at red lights is an awesome time to pray. Not only do you have to wait, which is patience, but you have time now. In the world, there's a lot of what I call "dead time": walking down the street, going out in a park some time.

Marcus: I was thinking about people who stand in line and get frustrated — that's a great time to pray for patience.

Mother Angelica: Oh, yes, but it's a great time to say, "Well, Jesus, You know how we are. I'm kind of impatient now." Talk to Him honestly. We're always putting on some kind of act before God. You can't act before God. He knows you! The best thing to do is to look at God and say, "Lord, I am impatient. But I don't want to be. Give me patience." You're praying! And if you're driving down the highway, and it's not a busy time, you look around, and you say, "Lord, You're so wonderful. I mean, that mountain is so big, I mean, You're omnipotent. And You created it only with a desire. Let there be light or mountains or the sea." You see, I have to definitely call on the gifts of the Spirit to grow in the spiritual life. If I fear God, I want to be with God. So, I'm constantly fighting. You're constantly fighting something. That's the purpose, and that's the way to holiness. You just don't become holy by breathing in and out.

Marcus: I was wondering, Mother, as we draw to a close, and this connects with that person's question — given the fact that the fear of God is such an important part for the beginning, the stepping stone in the Beatitudes, what about those of us that may look at our spiritual lives and realize, "Well, my spiritual life didn't begin with a good, healthy fear of God. What do I do now?" How do people instill in their spiritual lives this cornerstone of their spiritual journey?

Mother Angelica: You have to ask for it. "Ask, and you shall receive" (see Matt. 7:7). You can be guaranteed that when you ask the Lord for anything deeply spiritual to unite you to the Father, you're going to get it, I guarantee it. You may not get the new car you want, but you'll get patience, love. And you need to know, "I need You, Lord." That act of humility will bring everything with it. You are in need, and only God can satisfy that need.

Marcus: Because actually at the kernel of that humility, when we humble ourselves before God, that is the fear of God.

Mother Angelica: That's right. It's the filial fear. Thank you for having me!

The Church Is the Family of God
Interview with Scott Hahn
(May 1998)

Marcus: Welcome to *The Journey Home*. My name is Marcus Grodi, your host for this weekly program, in which I have the great privilege of discussing with you people who have come home to the Catholic Church, who've gone through difficult journeys but at the end discovered the great joys and the wealth of blessings that are in this beautiful Church.

My guest is Dr. Scott Hahn. My guess is that most of you know Scott and have maybe read his books, tapes, or heard about his own journey. He and his wife, Kimberly, have both had a great influence on so many people's lives, opening up their hearts to the truth of the Catholic Church. From the beginning of *The Journey Home* program, I've wanted Scott to get on. It's been hard because of his schedule teaching, but I want you to welcome him with me as we talk about his journey to the Church. Scott, welcome to the show.

Scott: It's good to be with you finally.

Marcus: Who'd have thought that we'd be here on this Catholic television show at one point?

Scott: Eighteen years ago when we first met, neither of us could have predicted this, that's for sure.

Marcus: We would have thought we were crazy at that time. I presume our audience knows about your journey to the Catholic Church, but in case they don't, they can find a copy of your book *Rome Sweet Home* online. And it's based on your tape, which came out how many years ago?

Scott: It came out in '89, four years before the book did.

Marcus: So, it was almost ten years ago that your tape came out, and I remember when I was just beginning. I wasn't even open to the Catholic Church at that point. I was looking for answers. But I ran back into you, and your suggestion was, "Listen to the tape, it'll help you understand." In fifteen minutes of listening to that tape, I was in trouble.

And maybe share with the audience a bit about how that tape came about, because it has such a big impact on people's lives.

Scott: Let's see, I became Catholic in 1986, twelve years ago. Then I had two or three silent years, but I really enjoyed them. Kimberly wasn't Catholic yet, and I needed to really get to know the Church. I had to be enculturated. I had the opportunity to lead Bible studies locally and this sort of thing, but I didn't really get much attention, and I thank God for it. But in '89, I was in contact with the Franciscan University of Steubenville. Alan Schreck, the chairman of the chairman of the [theology] department at the time, was already making overtures, and I was prayerfully discerning my way to employment there with a lot of excitement.

At the same time, I was getting to know Karl Keating and Pat Madrid at Catholic Answers, and they were also offering me a position. I knew my direction was toward Steubenville, but I wanted to get to know these guys better, and so they flew me out, and we spent a great weekend together. At the end of it — Sunday night, it was — we went over to St. Francis de Sales with Fr. Marx, just an informal gathering of about thirty-five people, and I shared my testimony of how I became a Catholic.

At the last second, a fellow named Terry Barber — who was working part time with this apostolate at St. Joseph Communications — decided, "I'm gonna show up, and I'm gonna tape this talk." So, he did, and at the end of the talk, he comes running up and says, "My friend, this is going to bless a lot of people." And I thought, "Well, all right, it's a talk given to thirty-five people. Whatever the Lord wants to do." Well, a year later, he let me know thirty-five thousand copies of that tape had been distributed around the world, and now nine years later, our estimates are well over a million copies of that tape. It's staggering! Who'd a thunk it?

Marcus: It is amazing. It makes you realize the great power of the media that is in our hands, the gift of the media, if used for the purposes of God, and how it can change lives. I'm not sitting here to pat you on the back, Scott, but it's just amazing. You can't go very far without running into people who have heard about how the Lord has led you and Kimberly in a way you never dreamed.

And it's because you love Jesus Christ. That was the bottom line of that whole issue, what drew you to the Church.

Scott: Yeah, I did not know the attention was coming. I wouldn't have pushed a button, saying, "Yes, bring it on." I would have run from it. But we've had a sense all along that the Lord was asking us to share with others the exciting truth that I had come to discover, much to my own shock. And I think it's that shock factor, the fact that I was an anti-Catholic, studying, and then became a Catholic. That helps a lot of people who might not be as opposed to Catholicism as I was. But that's the way of the Lord. It's certainly not my plan.

Marcus: Well, you've been in the Church now about twelve years, and during these last twenty to thirty years, there've been a lot of conversions. In fact, even to the point of many calling it a phenomenon. I've even heard some call it a new Oxford movement. Some estimate that there's a greater number of conversions today than maybe ever since the Reformation. We don't have statistics on these numbers, but I think on the one hand, to many Catholics, it's a great surprise that so many are actually coming home, whereas some are kind of skeptical of those figures.

What do you think of the conversions to the Church? Do you see it as a phenomenon?

Scott: I see it as a supernatural phenomenon, the likes of which we've never seen, not since the Protestant Reformation. Though it's called a new Oxford movement, if you go back to the last century, 150 years ago, and you look at Cardinal Newman's conversion, you discover that along with Newman there came hundreds of other Anglicans into the Roman Catholic Church. But Anglicans converted largely because they discovered that the Anglican Church *wasn't* really the Catholic Church. So, they were already so close to begin with, and Newman's conversion carried them over the edge.

What's so spectacular about what's been going on for the last decade or so, and I think what makes this really a kind of divine trademark — this is clearly a work of God — is the fact that we're not dealing primarily with Anglicans or Orthodox. We're dealing primarily with Evangelicals, with Fundamentalists, with Pentecostals and charismatics — people who would have regarded conversion to the Catholic Church as plain unthinkable, like I did. It's being sold out to Jesus Christ, it's being a slave to the Scriptures, but it's also being open to the fact that we don't know the Bible as well as we often portray ourselves, and it's just going deeper and deeper into God's Word, and into more and more of an intimate friendship with Jesus, where you discover His power and you're open to surprises. And then suddenly one of the biggest surprises imaginable comes along: the Catholic Church is something that Jesus instituted.

Marcus: About five years ago, you and Kimberly and the Rylands helped me in the process. We developed this apostolate called the Coming Home Network, in which we specifically focus on these conversions of clergy, and that's a major part of this phenomenon, isn't it?

Scott: In fact, that is the distinctive feature. We're not just talking about Evangelical, Fundamentalist, charismatic, Pentecostal, and Protestant Bible Christians becoming Catholic. What's so striking is the number of *pastors* who have converted, pastors who commit a kind of social suicide; it's a professional act of sacrifice. While we're here in front of a camera talking about it, a lot of these men, as you well know, are bagging groceries, are looking for work, and at the same time, they will testify to anybody who asks them, that whatever they gave up, they can't even compare to what they've gained in the Church, and especially in the Holy Eucharist.

Marcus: I don't think a week goes by where I don't hear from a new clergyman. We recognize that many of them come for so many different reasons, from different places. Given all of that, from your study and reflection, twelve years in your contact with so many converts, what do you see as maybe the underlying thread? If you could summarize it all and point it out maybe to those old friends in the pastorate that maybe don't speak to us anymore. If you could somehow help them understand *why*.

Scott: That's a good question. That's very fair. I wouldn't presume to speak for the hundreds of pastors who have come in, or the hundreds who are praying and studying now, but I would reflect on my own experience and suspect that I have this in common with many of them, if not all of them. When I was not a Catholic, there was one basic reason why. I looked at the distinctive beliefs of Catholics—Mary, the saints, the sacraments, especially the Eucharist and the pope—and I said, "These detract from the work of Jesus Christ. These complicate the simple gospel."

And now on the other side of things, I look at Mary and the saints, the sacraments, the Eucharist, and the pope, and I'd have to say there's one basic reason why I accept them, and that is because I see in these nothing less than the work of Christ. So, on the one hand, I opposed it because I thought Jesus died on the Cross and all you got to do is repent and believe, and you're saved. It's simple, so why complicate it with all this claptrap and superstition? But the deeper you go with Jesus, the more you realize that He wants to introduce you to His Father and to the Spirit and to the saints and to a whole family. God's family.

You also discover that He didn't do this for Himself. God didn't create the world and send His Son to die on the Cross in order to get more glory for Himself. In fact, I think we'll all be shocked at the end of time to discover that after history is done, God did not end up getting a single drop more glory than what He had in the beginning. He had it all. So, He couldn't have created and redeemed the world to get more glory for Himself. He did it to *give* His glory. And that's a whole new way of thinking for me. Because I always thought of this idea of glory as a tug of war. If man gets glory, then God has to lose it. But the more you get to know God through Jesus Christ the Son, the more you see a Father, and the more you see salvation as a Father's work. A father is not threatened when his sons and daughters grow up and acquire his power, his knowledge, his goodness, his virtue. That's exactly how the Father glorifies Himself and lets the world know He's a good Father.

So, now I look at Mary, and I see the work of Jesus Christ. She doesn't take away from the work of Christ. She doesn't detract from the light of Christ. She refracts that light. She is the masterpiece of Jesus, and the saints along with her. And I can only believe the sacraments because I believe in God's sovereign power. But it isn't just sovereign power; it's sovereign omnipotent love. So, as Father, He loves His family through His Son in the Spirit, through Mary, our

Mother, through the saints as our older brothers and sisters, and through these family rituals we call sacraments. All these other means at our disposal are in no way detracting from the work of Christ. They exemplify them.

And to me, this isn't just a rhetorical strategy; this isn't just an effective way to present the Faith so that non-Catholics who think a lot about God's glory, who think a lot about the work of Christ, will not be offended. This is the center and the heart and the soul of what we believe and how we believe it and why we believe it as Bible-believing Catholic Christians.

Marcus: A couple of questions. Why is it that our separated brethren would be so offended? Where did that come from? After fifteen hundred years and the honoring of so many faithful Catholic rituals and sacraments, how is it that all of a sudden the tide would turn, and it would be seen as a curse, as taking away from Christ? Can you explain where that would have come from?

Scott: Well, there's no simple answer. There are several factors. One of them is certainly the scandalous behavior of many Catholics. As I grew up, the Catholics I knew were all characterized by one trait: they were the ones who could swear more than me, drink more than me, and get in more trouble than me, and they led me astray. So, when I first converted and discovered Jesus Christ as my personal Savior and Lord, I didn't know any Catholics who shared that experience except ex-Catholics. So, I had no experience. Now, twelve years into this, I have met lovers of Christ the likes of which I never knew as an Evangelical. They're hidden, they're humble, but they're out there radiating the love of Christ, and I know you've met them too.

But I would also say this, that Western culture for the last six hundred years has become individualistic and experiential. It has rejected all of these things that are associated with the Middle Ages — hierarchy, tradition, authority, kingship, fatherhood, this sort of thing. And I would say that our culture doesn't prepare us to even begin to comprehend the Catholic Church, because the Catholic Church is based on this notion of the family of God. For us, the best we can do in respect to family is Mom, Dad, and the kids, and we pray they stay together. But when you look into the Bible, the biblical worldview is familial, family centered. But the family that God was fathering down through the ages wasn't just Mom, Dad, and the kids. When you look at Israel, it had twelve tribes, hundreds of clans, and thousands of families, but they understood themselves to be one family under God — the covenant family of the living God. When Jesus Christ came to establish the New Covenant, He didn't do away with this national family unity. He fulfilled it. He enlarged it. He made it an *international* family unity. The Greek word for that is *katholikós*, the Latin is *catholicus*, and the English word is *catholic*. The catholicity of the New Covenant is the defining feature of what Jesus Christ did.

I was in a conversation a few weeks ago with a Protestant friend of mine who was in my church. And I said, "You know, I could be wrong." I mean, humanly speaking, I've made mistakes. Just for argument's sake, I said to my friend, "I could be wrong about Mary and the saints, the Eucharist and the sacraments, the pope, and all the rest. And you could be right. But if I'm wrong, there's basically one reason why: because I'm giving Jesus Christ too much credit." I'm crediting Jesus for having made His Mother immaculate, like anybody would want to make their mother if they could. I'm giving Jesus all the credit for the infallibility of the pope, as well as the infallibility of the Scriptures. I'm giving Jesus Christ all the credit for empowering the saints as our intercessors, our older brothers and sisters, the Eucharist, and all the rest. So, if I'm wrong, the one thing I would expect to hear on judgment day is St. Peter saying, "You're wrong, but you're wrong because you gave Jesus too much credit." And I would say: "Guilty as charged!" That's the one accusation I could live with.

Marcus: This reminds me of the truth of John the Baptist's statement: "He must increase, but I must decrease" (John 3:30). That is the underlying self-surrender, self-conviction, that's at the center of all there is that's Catholic—whether it's Mary or the pope or the Scriptures—it's God at the center. And it's not just God, it's God the Father.

I know that what you're talking about is a passion for you, and it's expressed in your newest book, *A Father Who Keeps His Promises: God's Covenant Love in Scripture*. God the Father. Salvation means knowing the Father. Talk about that—knowing the Father.

Scott: I think about my own life and my own family. My kids know me as a teacher, as a traveler, as a professor, as a colleague, they see all the relationships that I have, but I tell them, "Dr. Hahn is what I do. Dad is who I am." So, I say to my kids, "You know me in terms of my own personal identity in a way that my students don't, in a way that people who would buy our books and listen to tapes couldn't possibly." And I think it's absolutely essential for us not to stop at what God has done for us but to move on to who He is. I know from my own experience, and you do too, how you feel when somebody only relates to you in terms of what you can do for them. Chances are you feel used. Now, that's okay if the person's an employee or an infant or a child or some dependent. But if they're not, then there's no real relationship possible, no friendship possible, unless that person is willing to get to know you in terms of your own personal identity. Not just in terms of what you've done for them or what you can do for them.

This came home to me, as far as God's concerned, one Sunday morning when I was at a parish in the Midwest. Up next to the priest was a woman, and she began the Mass, making the Sign of the Cross and saying, "In the name of the Creator, the Redeemer, and the Sanctifier." And I felt something in my gut give, and it wasn't simply: "Oh, this is politically correct." It wasn't that. I thought: "There's something even more wrong about that. What is it?" And I asked the Holy Spirit for light, and something hit me that it's okay to call God Creator, Redeemer, and Sanctifier. But those are things that God *does*. They're not who He *is*. In other words, how old is the creation? Some people might think it's thousands of years, other people might think billions or trillions of years, but we know one thing: creation is not eternal. But God is. So, whoever God is, He cannot be reduced to Creator because then His identity would be dependent upon creation, which it can't be, because God is whatever He is *before* He created. All the more, He cannot be reduced to redemption and sanctification. God *is* our Creator, Redeemer, and Sanctifier. But that's what He does. Not who He is.

John Paul II put it this way: "God in his deepest mystery is not a solitude, but a family, since he has in himself father-

hood, sonship and the essence of the family, which is love
[that is the Holy Spirit]."[3]

Notice that John Paul did not say "God is like a family."
He said God *is* a family, God is the only perfect family.
Drawing from the Holy Father's statement, I would say the
Hahns are like a family, because we have fatherhood and
sonship in my family, but it's only imperfect. Whereas in
God, the essence of the family is there in eternal perfection.
So, that is Who God is.

The Trinity is a doctrine that so many Christians
believe simply to avoid heresy, because they don't want to
go to Hell, they don't want to be guilty of heresy or false
teaching. But the Trinity is the center of our Faith. It's the
highest mystery of our Faith because it alone captures Who
God is eternally. John Paul II set aside 1997 for Jesus the
Son, '98 for the Holy Spirit, '99 for the Father, all in preparation for the jubilee. The year 2000 is a celebration of God
the Blessed Trinity. Why not God the Creator, Redeemer,
and Sanctifier? Because the Trinity is Who God is. And you
can't understand why God created, much less why He
redeems and sanctifies us, unless you see all of what He
does in terms of who He is. And everything that God does
is fatherly. Through Jesus the Son, in the Spirit, we become
sons and daughters of God, and the family of God.

In our individualistic society, that doesn't fit. It's hard to
understand.

Marcus: I was just thinking how one of the most common
questions that many people get at their door is "Are you

[3] John Paul II, Homily at Palafox Major Seminary, Puebla de Los
Angeles, Mexico (January 28, 1979).

saved?" From a Catholic perspective, the answer to that question lies in all you've just been talking about. And when we change our description of God to Creator, Redeemer, or Sanctifier—when we think we're going to make a better description of that salvation—we actually lose the essence of what our understanding of being saved means.

Scott: It's great to thank God for what He's done. That's thanksgiving. It's a perfectly appropriate form of worship, but it's a lower form of worship than what we call praise. We praise God for Who He is. We thank God for what He's done, and we only understand what He's done when we understand it in the light of Who He is. Salvation is not just being saved from sin. Sure, we're saved from sin, we're healed from its disease, we're forgiven from its penalty. But more than that, understanding this in radically trinitarian terms—that sounds lofty, but John Paul II wants Joe Six-Pack in the pew to understand, to contemplate, and to enjoy God the Father, Son, and Holy Spirit. So, this means we're not just saved from sin, we're not just saved from guilt, we're not just saved from Hell. We're saved *for* divine sonship.

We only experience the reality of salvation to the degree that we experience divine sonship. We call God *Abba*—Papa, Father. And we come to know ourselves as beings that we could not have made ourselves. We couldn't possibly buy our way into God's family. We couldn't work our way into God's family. You couldn't even work your way into *my* family. No kid could. It's a gracious gift. But it's the reality of salvation.

So, when people say, "Do you have a personal relationship with Jesus Christ?" I say, "Yeah, absolutely." "As your Lord and Savior?" "Yes!" But it's much more than that. I have a personal relationship with my car mechanic. But Jesus wants a covenant relationship. He wants a family bond. He wants to introduce God to us as Father.

Marcus: You've emphasized the fact that approaching theology from the right perspective makes all the difference to where you end up. If you approach it with different presuppositions, you're going to end out in left field. It's the same thing for the understanding of the words we use. For example, there's a verse in 1 John where it says the reason he's writing this is "that you may have fellowship with us; and our fellowship is with the Father and with his Son Jesus Christ" (1 John 1:3). He's not talking about coffee and donuts and going bowling. That's not what *fellowship* is. We're talking about union with God, an intimate walking with God, in which we become like Him. And truly, He comes in us—His divine life, His grace—He comes and changes us from the inside out. That's what it means about being born again. By Baptism, we're new people—but we're not just wiped clean; we're children of God. All in a family.

Scott: 1 John 3:1, "See what love the Father has given us, that we should be called children of God; and so we are." But you know, it's one thing to be called a child of God, it's another thing to actually *be* a child. See, I loved my dog Sparky growing up, a little Shetland Sheepdog. If I could have, I probably would have adopted him as a brother, but I couldn't. Not only because I didn't have a legal authority, but because if I had a legal authority, I couldn't have exercised that legal authority in any way to make him a family member, because family members necessarily share the same nature. But that's why 2 Peter 1:4 says we have "become partakers of the divine nature." God isn't just interested in forgiving us. Yes, He wants to forgive, He wants to heal us. But the Catholic doctrine of salvation is wrapped up in this Greek word *theosis*. The early Church Fathers used that to describe divinization, deification. We are transformed from sinful creatures into loving sons and daughters of the Most High God. That isn't just a name; that is our everlasting identity. Our earthly families are transitory; they're fading away. The divine family is our only true eternal home. If we could just enjoy this, if we could study it as Catholics, if we could encourage each other to come to understand this more and more, I'm convinced we would have a renewal that would look more like an explosion.

Marcus: It's just claiming our birthright. What did Jesus say? We must become like children. It makes sense, doesn't it?

Scott: If we could convey this to people, then Protestants would look at the Christian faith and say, you know, if it really is a trinitarian and fatherly work, then for there not to be a Mother, for there not to be saints, for there not to be sacraments, for there not to be a Holy Father as in a pope, or spiritual fathers as in priests—any Bible Christian would look at this, they would say, "That would be odd for these things not to be there!"

Marcus: We've got a bunch of calls waiting. Before I jump in though, we had one kind of hanging question that I really want to make sure we get to, and that is kind of the practical application of all that you've said. How do we bring this down and apply it in people's lives to help them experience and appreciate the childhood that they've been given through grace?

Scott: I think the one area, practically speaking, where this could make the biggest difference in the world is with our own assurance, our own personal assurance of salvation. I'm not talking about the false certitude that non-Catholics often claim presumptuously to possess and to know with a certainty that it's there.

Marcus: And push Catholics to claim for themselves.

Scott: That's right, and make it almost indispensable for true salvation, which it isn't. But on the other hand, Catholics often act as though they have no basis for assurance of salvation, when in fact they do. This is wrapped up with the theological virtue that we memorize as children. You've got faith, and you've got love, but you've got the neglected virtue of hope. Hope is this assurance that we possess. But I got to tell you, it came slow, it came long and hard for me.

When God conferred the dignity of fatherhood upon me—He's done it five times so far with five of the most wonderful kids in the universe—when He gave those five kids to me, He gave an additional gift I didn't know at the time, and that was the gift of assurance. Because I became certain of one thing: I can't possibly love my kids more than God loves His. And it does me so much good to think about that. I can't love my kids more than God loves His. And I can't begin to describe how much I love my kids.

Sometimes I still have doubts, sometimes I still need assurance, and I approach the Lord in prayer and say, "How do I know I'm your kid? I know abstractly that You love Your children more than I love mine, but how do I know I'm one of them?"

And typically, the Holy Spirit turns that question around and says, "Well, how do your kids know that they're your kids?" And you think for a second, "Well, that's easy." First of all, they live in my house. Second, they're called by my name, they're all Hahns. Third, they sit at my table. Fourth, they share my flesh and blood. Fifth, my bride, Kimberly, is their mother. Sixth, we're always celebrating together — birthdays, anniversaries, and vacations. And seventh, I discipline them. I don't discipline the neighbor's kids.

The Holy Spirit takes those seven and says, "Okay, Scott, look into My Word." And what do you find? "First, you live in My house." In Ephesians 2 and Hebrews 3, the Church that Jesus established, the one worldwide Church, is God's household.

"Second, you're called by My name, Scott. At Baptism, you were called by the name of the Father, Son, and Holy Spirit. I call you My child. You call God, *Abba*. Third, you sit at My table." The Lord was sitting at the table when He instituted the Eucharist. The Mass is when we gather as God's family and we sit at His table. "Fourth, you share My Flesh and Blood," the Lord says to me, "because that's Holy Communion."

"Fifth, My Bride is your Mother." The Church is the Bride of Christ, but it's *Mater Ecclesia*, it's Mother Church. Sixth, we're always celebrating together. Especially as Catholic Christians, the feast days and holy days of obligation, Advent and Lent, and everywhere you turn, you see another saint being celebrated, or the Blessed Virgin Mary as our family's Mother.

And seventh, the Lord disciplines us. Not only through our sufferings but especially through the Sacrament of

Reconciliation. He uses a man who has consecrated his life to be a spiritual father to give divine fatherly love and counsel and forgiveness. That's why the priest says, "I absolve you in the name of the Father, Son, and Holy Spirit," because that's family reconciliation.

So, I would say this: Catholics, lay hold on this birthright. Claim these grounds for assurance because I don't give my kids more solid grounds for assurance than God has given His. God has given us even greater grounds for assurance that we are His beloved children than any parent has ever given their children.

Marcus: Here on the set is a picture of the returning prodigal son to the father. It is always an image of a father with open arms, and it's there for us. Hearing you talk about that, I'm looking forward to reading your new book.

Scott: Well, this book is just a handy guide to the Bible so that Catholics can read it and get the big picture. I spend a lot of time making Leviticus make sense and come alive. Deuteronomy. The Apocalypse. The Gospels. Showing how the Old Testament is fulfilled in Jesus and how the Catholic Church is the embodiment of this fulfillment.

Marcus: Let's go to this email here and bring our audience into the discussion: "Dear Marcus and Scott. In *Rome Sweet Home*, Kimberly wrote about the difficulties when Scott was moving toward the Church. How did Scott pray for Kimberly when your journeys were at different paces? How should spouses pray, and what should they do when the other spouse is opposed to the journey?"

Scott: Number one, I would stop arguing. It took me a year to learn that lesson. Number two, I tried to live my faith with as much love, excitement, and enthusiasm as possible. Spurgeon once said, "If you want to attract the crowd, set yourself on fire." Well, it's true for spouses too. If you really want to attract them to Christ, or to the Church that Christ founded, don't set them straight, don't argue, don't harangue. Just live it with more love than ever before, and you'll become contagious.

I would also say the Rosary. If Mary is our Queen Mother, as we know her to be, then she loves your spouse more than you do, and she's also able to do more about it than you are. Go to her and say, "This is your child as well as my spouse. Love my spouse through me as only a mother can."

Marcus: Excellent. Let's take our first caller. This one comes from Palos Heights, Illinois. What's your question for us?

Caller: I wanted to ask Scott about calling Catholics to be Bible Christians and vice versa. I think it was in the last tape where he talked about praying the Mass and invoking the Lord's power in our lives. I just would like him to expound on this a little bit, that God would move in history and move in our lives when we live and pray the Mass the way it really should be prayed and attended. When I heard it, I was so overwhelmed because it really touched me, and I'd truly like to know if Scott could go a little further on that."

Scott: Oh, don't get me started. I would say this in a nutshell, if I can compress it. Reading the book of Revelation has been a pastime for me for more than two decades, and I've moved through every interpretive position out there.

But the one thing that has made the most sense out of it is to notice that every single time a judgment of God is announced in the Apocalypse, it's always in response to a song or to a prayer or to some liturgical activity that takes place in one of the two halves of the Apocalypse. The first half, you've got the Lamb breaking open the seals and revealing the contents of the book—the book of life, the sealed book. The second half of the Apocalypse climaxes in the marriage supper of the Lamb.

When you read the early Church Fathers, they saw this two-part movement as reflecting the Mass: the Liturgy of the Word and the Liturgy of the Eucharist. And the more you look into the Apocalypse, everything that happens—you have "Amens," you have "Alleluias," you've got "Worthy is the Lamb," you've got the "Holy, Holy, Holy," you've got "Lamb of God," *Agnus Dei*, you've got the incense, you've got priests dressed in linen, you've got prayers and songs and antiphons, you've got music being celebrated—if you take this to a Catholic and say, "What do you identify this with?" They'll say, "The Mass!"

Now, even to Catholics who don't read the book of Revelation—and I would say most Catholics avoid it unfortunately, but it was in studying the book that I realized—this is a depiction of how in the Mass we participate in the worship of the heavenly Jerusalem, with all the angels and saints gathered around the throne of the Lamb, Jesus Christ, Who is the King of Kings. This gives us our compass bearings so that when we are in the Mass, and we read the book of Revelation, we realize this is the activity that releases the power of God. If that's the case, if all of God's judgments, all of His deliverances are in response to the songs and the prayers offered in union with the Lamb's self-offering, then we ought to be inserting ourselves into the Mass as intelligently and as deliberately and as fervently as possible.

Marcus: What's the old phrase? In the Mass, we serve with the priest. We are taking part.

Scott: We are not spectators. We are co-offering this sacrifice in union with the priest. We serve at the altar of the Lamb. We could release so much spiritual power for our families and our society if we did that.

Marcus: Let's go to this next email: "Dr. Hahn, I am a recent convert to the Church. My two teens were received into the Church this Easter Vigil. My husband feels that the step we have taken wasn't a necessary one. Is this true?"

Scott: It's only unnecessary if Jesus never said, "On this rock, I will build my church." Unfortunately, my Bible has that in Matthew 16:18. So, it tells us that there is a Church that Christ has built and that Christ swore He'd maintain it over and against the gates of Hades, which would not prevail against it. He didn't say it was the pope's church. He didn't say it was the Catholics' church. He said, "It's My Church."

And if you look into the background of Matthew 16, you'll discover He couldn't possibly be talking about some invisible organization of like-minded people who had similar experiences. He's talking about a covenant family that is organized in terms of covenant doctrine, covenant worship, covenant morality, and really, there's only one applicant for the job. When I went searching for the fulfillment of Jesus' promise, because I knew He would not leave that promise unfulfilled, I found that there's only one church that claims to be worldwide, is age-old, and transcends all cultures and nations. It isn't just Lutheran, or Greek or Russian or Ruthenian. This is third-world, first-world, second-world. This is for Jews and Greeks. All of us are brothers and sisters in Christ.

Marcus: There's not another church in the world whose leader could have had an impact on Cuba, the way our pope could get every radio station broadcasting his message of the gospel.

Scott: Eastern Europe, too, back in the '80s, the Iron Curtain.

Marcus: It's just amazing. Let's take this next call from Norristown, Pennsylvania. Hello, what's your question for us?

Caller: First, I want to tell you that this is blessing from the Holy Spirit because I've had this on my heart, and I'm very privileged to talk to both you and Scott, and I want you both to know what a blessing you are to the Catholic Church. My question is to Scott. Would you please explain in detail what are the requirements of entering into the New Covenant in terms that a non-Catholic would readily receive?

Scott: This is a biblical question because you have to look into the Bible and find out what you have to do to enter into covenant commitments, covenant bonds. And you discover that you've got to make promises, but the promises are not enough. A promise makes a *contract*, but a *covenant* depends upon an oath being sworn. Because in a contractual relationship, my word is my bond, and that word is my name. But in a covenant relationship, God is the cement that binds people's lives together, and the only way you can form covenants is through oaths that are sworn. Now, that's a strange thing for Americans, because oaths are not things that we're familiar with. I mean, we swear them, but we don't really understand them. It's important, though, to realize that from the very beginning, since Jesus and the apostles established the New Covenant, the Church as the family of God, He left us oaths. Where are these New Covenant oaths? Well, the Latin word for oath is *sacramentum*. The sacraments of the Catholic Church are the oaths of the New Covenant.

If you make a simple equation, *oath* translated into Latin is *sacramentum*. Then the way you enter into covenant is through sacraments. So, the way you enter into God's family is through the sacraments, beginning with Baptism, and on we go.

Marcus: We talk about this change that happens in our life as we surrender ourselves to the New Covenant: we're changed, Christ changes us, the old is gone and the new has come. I've been thinking, as we've changed in our journey into the Catholic Church, that part of it has come from discovering the fullness of the Faith, and sometimes when we see others that aren't experiencing and appreciating it, we wish they would. And I was just thinking earlier about your "Joe Six-Pack in the pew" comment. What do we mean by that?

Scott: We mean the average Catholic who doesn't necessarily strike his colleagues as a devout disciple of Jesus Christ. This really fits with our caller's question too, because you've got to realize that a covenant is something that people can belong to without appreciating it, without even knowing it. So, you have to emphasize the sacraments on the one hand but never to the neglect of personal faith, personal repentance, and personal conversion. The sacraments don't replace those personal actions; they reinforce them. And so, we need to make our promises to God, we need to make our peace with God, we need to repent, and believe in Jesus Christ, but we also have to recognize that all that we do on our own isn't enough. We have to have God kick in the rest.

But I also want to add this: the Joe Six-Pack in the pew can often be more of a true believer than Evangelicals recognize because, though he doesn't necessarily talk the talk, he might walk the walk in a quiet way.

Marcus: Real quickly, another email: "Dear Scott. I missed the pilgrimage you and Kimberly led to the Holy Land. Do you have any plans to lead another trip there?"

Scott: Yes, we do — and I can't find a word to describe it. It's a life-changing experience when you read the Bible after having been in the Holy Land. It's three-dimensional. It comes to life. It just jumps on the center stage and sings and dances. We've been in touch with a lot of people who were with us on the pilgrimage a couple of years ago, and their lives, like ours, were changed forever.

Marcus: With all that you've said, isn't the underlying reason for it all that we might become saints? Isn't that the calling, the journey? It isn't just becoming Catholic that we talk about. What does it mean to become a saint as the ultimate goal of all that we're called to in following Christ?

Scott: When we talk about conversion, we're not talking about becoming Catholic, because that isn't the end. That's a means to the end. Conversion has for its end only one thing: Christ-likeness, sanctity, holiness. Conversion can never be reduced to just external membership in the Roman Catholic Church, as beautiful and as powerful as that is. Conversion is always and only associated with my repenting of the sin that has blocked God's love in my life, my recognizing my weakness, acknowledging, like the prodigal son: "I am not worthy to call You Father, I'm not even worthy to be Your servant, and yet because of Your omnipotent love, this unfathomable mercy, it's almost too good to be true" (see Luke 15:19). But it isn't too good to be true. It's too good to have been invented by man. And this to me is what conversion is all about.

John Paul II said this: "Become a saint, and do so quickly." Don't waste your life. Don't say, "Well, I'll do it when I get old. I'll have all the fun I can have in the world now, and then I'll be a saint later." No, your heart will be hard. But besides that, you can't have more fun, you can't possibly have more fun or joy or peace than what the saints possess. The only thing we're on earth for is to become a saint.

Marcus: When we talk about the journey home, even in the work that we do together on the Coming Home Network, we've often said that our primary goal is not making everybody Catholics; it's helping them become saints.

I was reminded of one of the greatest comments my five-year-old said about me. He was doing something in the yard, and I overheard him. He didn't know I was there, and he was singing this little song he knew, and he was singing, "I wanna be like my dad, I wanna be like my dad." And I choked up.

Scott: That's sanctity. Becoming like God.

Marcus: That's what it's all about! We're called to be like our Dad—by God's grace. We don't do it alone.

Scott, thank you so much for being on this show. It's always a great joy, and I hope to have you back. God bless you and Kimberly and the family.

Dr. Scott Hahn has been reminding us of something we may very often take for granted, and that is the great, great benefit we've received by God's freely given grace that has made us, undeserving as we are, His children, and that brings with it all the blessed benefits that come from being a part of His family. And that's why Jesus can call us to love even our enemies, to love one another. Because we're family. Sometimes people in the family rub us the wrong way, just like they do in earthly families. But we're called to love one another.

And that love with which we love is a gift of His grace. Our Father gives us all the tools we need to encourage, to equip, to empower, to lift up, to console, even to challenge. In Mass today, we had a wonderful homily that reminded us what love is all about, and in that homily, the priest reminded us that true love means saying the words that need to be said, even if they're difficult words. What is to come out of us and is to overflow from our lives is the great gift of God's love.

How does a spouse or someone else understand what it means to be a Christian? They should see it overflowing from our lives. We're together on the journey. May God be with you as we walk together in His grace, loving one another as brothers and sisters in the family of God. God bless.

The Church Is the Kingdom of God

Interview with Scott Hahn
(September 1999)

Marcus: Welcome to *The Journey Home*. It's a great privilege to have a friend on the program, Dr. Scott Hahn.

Scott, I could spend the whole program thanking you for all that you've done in my life and in your own witness, and I know so many others thank you for that. And on the one hand, I would presume that a good number of our audience knows your journey, but I'm going ask you to give a thumbnail sketch. Before we go there, what else is going on right now in your life?

Scott: Well, three days ago, a new semester began at Franciscan University in Steubenville, and I'm getting to teach an overload this time in addition to a graduate course on sin, conversion, and evangelization. I have a course in the theology of the Church and three sections of Principles of Biblical Study. So, it is great to be back in the saddle again. I'm also privileged to serve on a kind of dream team called the Missionaries of Faith with Jeff Cavins. We're doing a Bible study, *At Home with the Word*, on their website. I'm also working closely with Pat Madrid and his new venture, Basilica Press. You did a book, *Millennium Insurance*, with my wife Kimberly. I'm also working closely with *Envoy*. Matt Pinto is now the editor of *Envoy*, and I have a newsletter called "Scripture Matters" in every issue. I also have a radio show called *Scripture Matters* for their program *Right Here, Right Now*.

Then I have a book coming out in a couple of months called *The Lamb's Supper: The Mass as Heaven on Earth*. It's kind of an easy-breezy, down-to-earth guide to the Mass from the perspective of the book of Revelation. I take the thing that Catholics know the best and interpret it in the light of the book of the Bible that perhaps they know the least, and hopefully it's an exciting experience. I've heard many, many good things from people.

Marcus: It sounds like for you, coming home to the Catholic Faith is just kicking up and relaxing.

Scott: And not doing a thing! Not exactly.

Marcus: Give us a thumbnail sketch of your journey.

Scott: I was raised in a nominally Protestant family. I got into a lot of trouble. I was saved by the grace of God working through Young Life, and in the process, I came to love Our Lord in the Scriptures, most especially. But I was also trained by people who had staunch anti-Catholic convictions and who successfully imparted them to me. I became a very ardent anti-Catholic, and when I went into Young Life and then ministry, I carried those anti-Catholic convictions out. But more than being anti-Catholic, I was in love with Scripture, and so I went deeper and deeper over a decade or more. I came to the conclusion that the covenant, which is at the heart of God's Word and God's plan, is not a contract. It's a family bond that reflects God's own Fatherhood, Christ's own Sonship, and the family oneness that the Holy Spirit brings about. I was fathering a family for the first time in my life, and I could see the need for a father to keep his family one. I looked around, and I saw twenty-six thousand denominations, and I wondered, "Okay, is the Father falling asleep at the wheel or what?"

It really set me on a long, hard search, and afterward I found about 101 things that all came up Catholic. So, I left the ministry, I quit teaching, I went into doctoral studies full-time. In 1986, I entered the Catholic Church, and in 1990, my wife, Kimberly did too. That's it.

Marcus: I never would have dreamed that the Lord would have given an apostolate to me to be working with others, and in some ways, it's your journey that's led to others, and many of us have come in.

Scott: It seems like yesterday that you walked up to me and shocked me at that church in Cleveland. I was giving a talk on the Eucharist, "The Fourth Cup," and you were there, and I didn't know why. You said, "I saw your name in the paper; I wondered what's he doing, so I came to see."

Marcus: I came to figure out if it was true, the rumors I had heard that you had lost your mind. And then you sold me a copy of your tape. But you charged me more than they did at the table.

Scott: Well, you were a Protestant.

Marcus: Ha!

Scott: I didn't charge you a thing!

Marcus: I went to listen to the tape to figure out where you went wrong, and within fifteen minutes, I was in trouble. In your expression of the problems of *sola Scriptura* and *sola fide* especially.

Scott: I think that was the issue for me. The most powerful change was discovering that as hard as I looked and as deeply as I struggled, I could not find anywhere that Scripture taught that the Bible is our only source of divine revelation in some authoritative way. The Bible kept pointing me to the living Tradition that stemmed from Christ and the apostles, and the teaching authority that Christ invested His Church with, especially the apostles and their successors. So, for me, being a Bible Christian required me to become a Catholic.

Marcus: You were set up. You relied so much on the Bible and then realized, "Where does it say this in the Bible?"

We might get a question on that later, but I want to ask you another question. I know there are plenty of emails and probably phone calls all ready to come with questions that they'd like to ask you, but I want to pose one question to kind of prime the pump a little bit from maybe a devil's advocate perspective, to ask a question to you as if I were a non-Catholic. And I feel as I'm asking this question that I'm just peeking into a fire hydrant, about to get blown across the room. But the question is this, and I get this a lot in different ways: When you look back at your reason for becoming Catholic, many of us become Catholic because we believe that the Church is the pillar and foundation of truth and that one of the claims is that the Church from the beginning to the end has not changed her teachings. But often we'll get letters from Protestants that will point to different places, saying, "Well, they changed this position there, and here or here," and I could name a couple places where they claim that.

But there's one that I'd like to bring up, that I know is close to your heart. It seems that in the past, Catholic teaching, the writings of authorities, and the Church teachers in the Church as well as laity and priests were much bolder about claiming that the Catholic Church is equivalent to the Kingdom of God. We see the expression "Kingdom of God" in Scripture, and it's pointing to the Catholic Church. Whereas it seems that today the teachers, the speakers for the Church, the theologians, have turned almost 180 degrees to almost dis-claim that, and some would say, "Hey, the Church changed her teaching."

Scott: It's a good question. First of all, we have to recognize that when we affirm the identity of the Church's teachings today and the continuity with the Church's teaching say in the first, second, and third centuries, we're not talking about a static uniformity; we're talking about a dynamic continuity. If you went back to my house tomorrow with me in Steubenville and you saw the way I was fathering my six kids—I've got two teenage boys and a beautiful twelve-year-old daughter named Hannah, and now a seven-week-old child who did not want to go to sleep last night from two-thirty until five—you would see how differently I father each one of those six kids. It's the same reality that I want to convey, and that is true love, virtue, unity, service, sacrifice, maturity. Yet you have to do it in different ways, even though

it's the same thing you're doing, and the differences that
emerge are because of the different time periods and the different circumstances.

I remember hearing an archbishop from Southeast Asia.
He was addressing a group of people who said, "Why did the
Church change this, that, and the other thing?" And one
lady said, "You didn't answer that guy's question! What
about the Friday discipline? Why did the Church get rid of
no meat on Friday?" And this archbishop said, "Ma'am, it's
because at Vatican II, for the first time in history, we had
more bishops representing the third world than the first
world. And in the third world, most of my people don't eat
meat Monday, Tuesday, Wednesday, or Thursday, so what
difference does it make if they can't eat it on Friday?" And
so, we were becoming truly Catholic in Vatican II—universal, international—and the disciplines were adjusted
accordingly. People in the West who kind of think that the
sun rises and sets in the West—Europe and America—didn't
comprehend. I thought it was a point well taken.

But I think if you go back, you'll recognize that this really
is an important issue. At the turn of the century, a French
biblical scholar named Fr. Loisy at the Catholic Institute in
France raised this question: How is it that Jesus promised the
Kingdom, but all He left us with was the Church? That really
bothered Loisy, so much so that he ended up losing his faith;
he ended up leaving the Church, losing his priesthood, and
dying an atheist excommunicated from the Church.

This is also a big thing among Fundamentalists who back
the Zionist return of Jews to Jerusalem and expect to be rap-
tured up in the clouds and expect that Jesus will come again
and set up a military theocracy in Jerusalem for a thousand
years. Why? Because all of these promises that Jesus made

seem to have gone unfulfilled. "Repent, for the kingdom of heaven is at hand" (Matt. 3:2). Well, it's been two thousand years now, Lord. With all due respect, what did You mean by "at hand"?

Well, I think the key is to recognize two things. First, what He says to Peter in Matthew 16. There He announces His intention to build the Church upon this rock. He doesn't say, "Peter, go build Me a Church, and I'll come back and check it out." He says, "On this rock I will build my Church" (Matt. 16:18). Peter happens to be the occasion, the person that Christ is going to work with. But Christ is the worker, and the Church is His. Peter and all the apostles are mere instruments in His hands. Then He goes on to say, "I tell you, you are rock, and on this rock, I will build My Church, and the gates of Hades shall not prevail against it." Why? "[Because] I will give you the keys of the kingdom of Heaven" (Matt. 16:19). He doesn't say, "When you die and you get to Heaven, I've got a gift for you, and that gift will be the keys of the Kingdom." No, Jesus entrusts them to Peter and through Peter to all the Twelve. Then in Matthew 19, He's already called the twelve apostles and He says they will sit on twelve thrones and judge the twelve tribes of Israel. That specifies that the Kingdom that Christ came to establish isn't just the reign of God in some generic sense of divine governance. I mean, God governs the world, God governs Venus and Jupiter, and so we speak of the rule of God or the reign of God. That's true no matter what—He's always been in charge. That's why I hesitate to affirm those translations, the modern versions, that say the "reign of God" or the "rule of God" or the "kingship." No, it is the Kingdom of God.

But more specifically, when you look closely, you'll see—and this is my second point—it's the *Davidic* Kingdom.

Matthew underscores Jesus' identity as the Son of David. In Matthew 1, we have the genealogy of Jesus, tying Him straight to David. And so, when Jesus comes proclaiming the Kingdom, it isn't just the divine governance, it is the Davidic Kingdom that united twelve tribes. This is what was so different about David's Kingdom as opposed to Moses' covenant with just the nation of Israel on Mount Sinai. David's Kingdom, as God made His covenant and kept it, united the twelve tribes *and all the Gentiles* under the Son of David. So Solomon comes and is endowed with God's wisdom. He builds a temple. He is the King of Israel. But he is the teacher of *all the nations.*

Now, that didn't last long. After forty years, it began to fall apart, but God made a covenant saying it will come back and it will last forever. So, when Jesus comes and He says, "Repent, for the kingdom of God is at hand" (see Mark 1:15) and then chooses twelve disciples, not seven—sacred as the number seven is—not ten, but twelve. He says, "You will sit on twelve thrones, judging the twelve tribes of Israel" (Matt. 19:28). And then He also gives the Great Commission to go out into all nations. Why? Because "all authority in heaven and on earth has been given to me" (Matt. 28:18). Of course. He's the Son of David. He is the King, but not only the King of Israel, because the Kingdom of David included Israel and *all* the nations. That's why the temple that Solomon built was so different from the tabernacle that Moses built. The temple had a big room, the Court of the Gentiles, so that all of the nations could come and pray, whereas the tabernacle had room only for the twelve tribes. So, Jesus comes to build His Church, and He gives the keys of the Kingdom to Peter, which are handed down to his successors. In the process, He gathers together the lost sheep of the house of Israel through

His disciples, but then He sends them out to *all nations*: "Go out to all nations—all nations—and make disciples of them" (see Matt. 28:19).

Marcus: We've scratched the surface of what I hope will be a future book. I can tell as we talked earlier, and even now, that this is the heart of your study now, and it's an exciting thing. And we encourage those who are listening to listen and pray more deeply when you read Scripture and you see references to the Kingdom and to understand it in a different way.

Scott: It dignifies our existence because we are children of the King. We have royal power, and it's such a privilege, we can't afford to neglect it.

Marcus: Let's take our first caller, from Virginia. Hello, what's your question for us?

Caller: My first question for Dr. Hahn concerns the possibility of salvation for those outside of faith in Christ. What I had in mind was a person who was from the tradition of Islam, for instance, who through no fault of their own never heard of Christ. Would it be possible—through, not an explicit faith in Christ, but an implicit faith in Christ, since we know that all salvation is through Christ, since He's the one true Mediator—for them to be saved? And if so, how does this affect our mandate for evangelism? Would it not be almost better for them not to have heard about Christ, if it's possible for them not having heard about Christ to be saved?

Scott: No, it wouldn't be better.

Marcus: I laugh just a little bit because I remember back in seminary, it seemed like we were on that question all the time, dealing with it from a Calvinist perspective, and you remember the Calvinists kind of lagged in their missionary zeal because of their conclusion to that question. And that conclusion is a bit different from ours as Catholics.

Scott: That's right. First of all, I would say that nobody's condemned to Hell because they never heard of Jesus Christ. You're only condemned because you've sinned against whatever light God has given you. The second thing I would say is that we are not into religious indifference or relativizing all religions and just saying, "Hey, what really matters is simply that you're a *sincere* Catholic or a *sincere* Buddhist." No. If there is a possibility for Muslims and Buddhists to be saved, it's not because of how sincere they were in practicing a religion that we are deeply convicted is riddled with mistakes, with errors, especially in overlooking the Son of God Who became a man, Who offered Himself for our sins. I think the third thing we want to say is that yes, people are saved apart from an explicit awareness of Jesus of Nazareth being their personal Savior. We know that's the case, at least in the Old Testament, where they simply had promises from God, they had assurances of His mercy, they knew that they were dealing with a God Who was kind and tender and willing to forgive, Who knew where they were. I mean, you've got a man like Job who wasn't even an Israelite, or Melchizedek, who wasn't in the family of Abraham, who actually precedes Abraham.

So, what really matters is what you do with the light that God gives you, that is what the judgment of God is going to be based upon, and you can be sure it will be just as well as merciful. But I would say this: the Catholic view of salvation is not reducible down to: "Are you gonna get out of the fires of Hell and make it into Heaven?" As important as that is, salvation is not reduced to a fire insurance policy or escaping damnation. Salvation is nothing less than being adopted into God's family.

I was on a radio program a couple of months ago, and I made a comment, just an offhand remark, where I said, "Salvation for Catholics in the Scriptures is more than mere forgiveness." The guy stopped and said, "More than mere forgiveness? What do you mean? Mere forgiveness? We're pardoned! We're forgiven! That's the gospel!" I said, "No. I mean we *are* forgiven, but it's more than mere forgiveness." "What do you mean?" I said, "Well, a month ago I took my car to get worked on, and it didn't go quite right. I went to this mechanic whom I had gone to for the first time, and I showed him a few weeks later how he didn't charge me correctly. He apologized, and I forgave him. But I didn't adopt him."

And that makes all the difference in the world. God has adopted us, and He has filled us with His own nature. 2 Peter 1:4, we have "become partakers of the divine nature." *Theosis* in the Greek means deification, divinization. So, the idea is, if we are in God's family, living in the Church, which is the universal family of God, then as His sons and daughters, we are experiencing the reality, the substance, the meaning of what salvation really entails. To be outside of the Church, in a sense, is to be outside of God's family. That's exactly what we need to be saved from. So, the essential meaning of salvation is more than a fire insurance policy, more than whether you're elected or reprobated. It's whether right now you are experiencing the fullness of life in Christ through the seven sacraments, in the family that He instituted through Peter and His apostles.

Marcus: I remember when I heard the tape that you produced on your conversion, and that verse in 1 John 3 jumped out at me because I'd never heard the understanding of salvation through those words. I mean, I've read it many times, I even helped write a commentary on 1 John, but for some reason it didn't hit me, when he says, "We [are] called children of God; and so we are." You made such a big emphasis on this, and it hit me. "See what love the Father has given us, that we should be called children of God; and so we are" (1 John 3:1).

Scott: Not just called children, but *made* children. And so we *are*. Not just so we're *called*.

Marcus: I remember, your emphasis on that made scales fall from my own eyes, and it brought me back into reading 1 John even more deeply. There's a verse a little earlier that reminds us in our missionary outreach why it is so important that we tell everyone about the fullness that is ours. It says in 1 John 2:28: "And now, little children, abide in him, so that when he appears we may have confidence and not shrink from him in shame at his coming." It's not just forgiveness. It's all that we are. We're called to grow in holiness so that we can one day stand before Him without embarrassment.

Scott: You know, if a Martian came to earth and, "Explain to me what human life is," we wouldn't go to an intensive care unit or an ER and say, "See that guy? He's hanging on. We still have a pulse. That's life!" No, that's a guy who's just barely alive. If we want to explain what life is, then we show it in terms of health and strength and intelligence. If we want to explain to people what salvation is, we point to the Trinity, and with the Holy Father, we say, "God in his deepest mystery is not a solitude, but a family, since he has in himself fatherhood, sonship and the essence of the family, which is love [that is the Holy Spirit]."[4] If that's Who God *is*, then *what* He's doing in giving us salvation is incorporating us into that trinitarian family life, and nothing less will really adequately explain what we mean by salvation.

Marcus: Excellent, Scott. I'm going to need to ask the producers to go into the backroom and see if we can extend the program a couple of hours.

Scott: Ha!

Marcus: We have so much that we'd love to cover. Let's take this email: "Dear Scott, like yourself, I was a former Presbyterian minister, ARP, and converted to the Roman Catholic Church. I have two questions. In the Catholic view, explain the difference between justification and sanctification. And two, please clarify the Assumption of our Blessed Mother, as I'm confused. Since she was sinless, did she die a different kind of death, that is, if she died at all since she was without sin? Did she ascend to Heaven like Jesus? Thanks."

Scott: First of all, I would say that justification in the historic Protestant sense is a judicial act. It is a divine decree, a courtroom judgment, whereby God declares us to be innocent on the basis of Christ's righteousness. It's an external, extrinsic sort of thing, where God imputes Christ's righteousness to us. As Catholics, we would say, "Yes, but there's more." We

---

[4] John Paul II, Homily at Palafox Major Seminary.

wouldn't put a period at the end, we'd put a comma and say that He doesn't just impute it legally, He imparts it sacramentally, so that we are made partakers of the divine nature. We aren't just legally declared to possess it, we actually do.

Justification and sanctification are like heads and tails of the coinage of salvation, and you wonder, "Well, aren't they the same sort of thing?" Well, no. If we understand what I was just mentioning a moment ago, that it's the Trinity Who saves us, the Father through the Son in the Spirit, then we recognize that we share the life of God, the Father, Son, and Holy Spirit. Well, that life comes to us through Christ, and that is justification. It's sharing Christ's sonship. That's how the Council of Trent defined justification in section 6, chapter 4, that it's being taken out of the old Adam through whom we lost our divine sonship and being reunited, incorporated with Christ as the New Adam so that we share in His divine sonship.

But it isn't just the Son's sonship, it's the Spirit's sanctity. That's sanctification. Because salvation is not just being saved from Hell but being made to partake of the Trinity's life, it has to consist of the sonship of Christ and the sanctity of the Spirit, and the Father confers both. The Catholic Church distinguishes the two, but it never does what we used to do in separating them.

A lot of times, we used to say, "Well, justification is what happens in the very beginning when you first have faith, and *then* sanctification follows." The problem with that is that nowhere does Paul say it. And if you try to get him to say it in Romans, he is using that famous text, Genesis 15:6, where Abraham believed and it was reckoned to him as righteousness, and God justified him. But that couldn't have been the moment when Abraham first came to saving faith because

Abraham was walking with God by faith already in Genesis 12, 13, and 14. He's been living by faith for many years. So justification is a process, not just a passing moment, just like sanctification.

Marcus: Maybe one of the biggest areas where we do differ, where we get a misunderstanding even from what you've just said, is that many outside the Catholic Church have accepted without question the idea that once you're justified, you're justified.

Scott: Many Catholics I find who might tune into the radio during rush hour, or watch television and see these televangelists, will come to me with questions, and I'll say, "Wait, before I can answer that question, I have to uproot some weeds in the garden here. You have some assumptions that are faulty." A lot of Catholics think in a confused way when it comes to justification.

Marcus: Let's take the second question: "Please clarify the Assumption of our Blessed Mother, as I'm confused. Since she was sinless, did she die a different kind of death?"

Scott: When we speak of Mary's Assumption and Christ's Ascension, what we differentiate is the fact that Christ by His own divine power ascended into Heaven, whereas Mary's Assumption is more of a reception of divine power. That is, she doesn't raise herself like Christ's Ascension. Christ is the one Who is raising her in the Assumption.

Now, what do we say about Mary dying? There are some who say she just fell asleep and others who say that she died but didn't experience corruption. I think you have to say in either case that she didn't undergo the corruption that we have as a result of the curse placed upon sinners. She was preserved from sin. I think you also have to get back to the heart and the soul of what the Church teaches about Mary, whether it's her bodily Assumption or her Immaculate Conception, that this is the work of Christ.

Being perfect Love, you'd expect Him to want to share at least part, if not all, of His glory. In fact, He wants to share *all* of His love, all of His glory. And being an omnipotent, all-powerful God, you'd think that His chances of success would be pretty great. Mary is Exhibit A, to show that it worked, to impart to us the fullness of His glory, and nothing less. Mary is the perfect expression of Christ's redemptive work; she is His greatest masterpiece. And so the more we make of her Assumption or her Immaculate Conception, the more we say, "Yes, Christ's redemptive work is perfect." Not that it added anything to Him, but it added everything to us, and it came to us through our Mother, His Mother, because we're His family.

Marcus: The Catholic Church has always taken that phrase "full of grace" to mean just what it says.

Scott: Exactly. It's a fullness of plenitude.

Marcus: Let's take our next caller, from Pennsylvania. Hello, what's your question for us?

Caller: My question is on Original Sin. You have two parents who are in the state of grace; they both made worthy Confessions; they consummate their marriage, and a child is conceived. So you have two parents in the state of grace and you have God Who is the author of all holiness. How is Original Sin then transmitted? Section 404 in the *Catechism* says that it is a sin which will be transmitted by propagation to all mankind. That's what I don't quite understand. How can God be the author of a weakened will or a weakened intellect?

Scott: This is an incredibly good question. I've never had this question before, but I'm addressing it in my seminar. And I must say, if Catholics don't get Original Sin right on the button, they almost invariably get everything else wrong, and most Catholics just get it just a little bit off, because they haven't studied the documents and the Scriptures enough to see how carefully defined the Church's teaching is. We often resort to metaphors when we think of Original Sin, like a stain that Baptism washes away. But it isn't a stain. No, actually, Original Sin is not anything. In fact, the way the Church carefully defines what Adam did in propagating our race with Original Sin, transmitting Original Sin, was that he *dis*-graced us. Where we needed grace, we lost it. And so, Original Sin is simply the *lack* of the very divine grace we need to achieve that which God made us for. That's what Baptism does in "wiping away" the stain of Original Sin. It's simply putting into our soul that which was lacking.

No matter how holy Kimberly ever gets, no matter how holy I might be, if we renew our covenant, that is a natural process that does not convey supernatural life. That is the means by which human life is propagated, but it's not the way divine life is transmitted, and it's divine life that we refer to by the word *grace*. So, grace is what we lost through Original Sin. We were dis-graced, we were disinherited from the share of divine sonship.

We have Original Sin without our consent, and so Baptism for infants restores grace without their consent. When we commit actual sins, we give consent, and so we must go to Confession and ask for forgiveness with consent. The Church has taught this so clearly, but unless you spend a little bit of time in the Scriptures and then the Fathers and then the official teachings of the Church, it's easy to just kind of lean on the metaphors or the figures of speech, like stain or corruption or whatever. Outside the Church, you will find a lot of real confusion, that Original Sin actually renders children guilty. The Church says no way! You can't be condemned for a sin you didn't commit.

Marcus: Let's take this email: "During the last year, God has put a burning desire in me to explore the depths of the Catholic Faith. The more I read the Church Fathers and the history of the Church, the more devoted I become. I have one problem. Being raised in a Protestant church, it is difficult to see the Real Presence of Jesus in the Eucharist. When I bow before the sanctuary and go to adoration, there is a hesitation for fear of worshipping the host and not Jesus. Do you have any scriptural confirmation for me?"

Scott: The first place I would go is the sixth chapter of John's Gospel. There Jesus says, not once, not twice, not even three, but *four* times, "Unless you eat the flesh of the Son of man and drink his blood, you have no life in you; he who eats my flesh and drinks my blood has eternal life.... For my flesh is food indeed, and my blood is drink indeed. He who eats my flesh and drinks my blood abides in me, and I in him" (John 6:53–56). I think that's enough right there to go on, but I would also look at the passages in 1 Corinthians 10–11. If we had more time, I would unpack Paul's explanation of how these Corinthians who have desecrated the Eucharist are, as a result, sick. Some have even died. Why? Because they've desecrated not just a symbol of that which is holy, but that which is substantially holy—the very Presence of Christ.

For me, the great experience was attending Mass for the first time and hearing four times in less than two minutes: "Lamb of God Who takes away the sins of the world, have mercy on us. Lamb of God ... Lamb of God ..." and then the priest said, "Behold the Lamb of God Who takes away the sins of the world." Suddenly, a light went on. I remember that in the Apocalypse, the book of Revelation, Jesus is called many things—Alpha and Omega, King of Kings, Lord of Lords, Lion of the Tribe of Judah—but He is called Lamb twenty-eight times in twenty-two chapters, which is more than all the other titles put together. In Holy Communion we have the marriage supper of the Lamb. The early Church Fathers loved to use that language to describe the second half of the Mass, which is the Liturgy of the Eucharist, the climax of which is Communion upon the Lamb of God.

I can't go into all the other things, but I must say this, that the book of Revelation, which I've been studying for twenty-two years, has now become, for me, not only the most Catholic book of the New Testament, but the most eucharistic. I pray that God's blessing will be upon readers who use *The Lamb's Supper* in reading the book of Revelation, because this book changed my life. It took me twenty years to think it out and twenty months to actually sit down and write it, but the result of it for me was the conviction that when I come before the Blessed Sacrament, it is the *parrhesia*—the Greek word for the Presence of Christ—the Real Presence. If we're lucky enough to be alive at the end of time and we see Christ coming on the clouds of glory, He will not have one drop of more glory then than He possesses right now in the Eucharist in our tabernacle.

Marcus: Another part of his question, besides the theology, was the practice of kneeling before what looks like a piece of bread and feeling in his heart the struggle with that issue.

Scott: The first time I had this interpretive breakthrough at Mass, I didn't stand once, and I certainly didn't kneel, and I most assuredly didn't genuflect. I sat there as an observer, like a journalist watching the whole thing. But after a few weeks, it dawned on me that if that is Who I think it is, as Kimberly put it years later, then it's not safe to refuse kneeling. If that is the Lord of Lords and the King of Kings, and He has assumed a form of bread and the appearance of wine so that we can receive Him not just in our souls and hearts but in our bodies ... I mean, you talk about the mercy of God. That takes mercy to a new limit. It's just incredible.

Marcus: I noticed by his message in the email that he was reading early Church Fathers, and I'd continue to do that because you'll see the early Church Fathers were totally convinced in the reality of Jesus in the Eucharist.

Scott: Especially St. Augustine. He says it's not a sin to bow and kneel before the Eucharist, but it is a sin not to.

Marcus: Let's take this caller from Maryland. What's your question for us?

Caller: I am a Lutheran clergywoman, and I am very much in agreement that there are so many conflicts in so many denominations, and I sense a oneness in the Roman Catholic Church and teaching, and it has been wonderful for me to partake of the Benedictine spirituality and many other things that have blessed me over the years. But there is still a great chasm regarding my understanding of my own deep call to ordained ministry and presiding at Eucharist and preaching and teaching in the Church. Why it is that the Catholic Church could not see that call when I know from deep within myself that it is so genuine?

Scott: I would address this at two levels. I would first look at my wife's experience, because when I first met her and I fell in love with her, she was bound and determined to be ordained as a Presbyterian, and she felt an undeniable call to ministry. After we studied Scripture together and after she did some research on her own, she came back to me with her head kind of hanging low, and she says, "You know, as much as I want it and as strongly as I feel called, I don't think I'm supposed to—just from the Bible." But then she had a deeper sense that, even though she's not called to the precise or specific form that we call ordination, she most assuredly was being called the whole time to minister to the Body of Christ sacrificially through the Word, in friendships and whatever other forms God gave her. What was so interesting was to see the revolution in her life. Because once she said, "Okay, God, I'll let go," I have never seen a woman on earth been given more opportunities to minister deeply to the profoundest needs of women as well as men.

The other thing I'd point out—and I have an article on the priesthood of the Old Testament in the *Encyclopedia of Catholic*

Doctrine published by *Our Sunday Visitor*—I do a careful study of the priestly actions of the patriarchs in Genesis and how being a father like Abraham, Isaac, and Jacob and being a priest were practically synonymous or interchangeable, so that by the time you get to Judges 17–18, you have a man who says to another fellow, "Will you be to me a father and a priest?" (See Judg. 17:10; 18:19). Well, which is it? Back then, these were two ways of saying the same thing, because to be a father means to sacrifice, to pray, to serve—that's what fatherhood entails. To be a priest is basically to spiritually father people. So, repeatedly in the book of Judges, you have this, "Will you be to me a father and a priest?" Well, once you put it together, you can understand why it is that the Church can't ordain women to be priests, because nature hasn't ordained them to be fathers. I heard one bishop say, "It isn't as though we don't want to. It's that we can't." We might ordain women to be priests the day after nature ordains them to be fathers. God the Creator and God the Redeemer are one and the same. The priesthood is spiritual paternity. There is an indispensable role for women. Spiritual maternity is just as important. But it's not what we mean by the sacrificial priesthood.

Marcus: I just have a thought, and I'm not aiming this at our caller at all, but in the work that I do with Protestant clergy who become Catholic or are on the journey to Catholicism, one of the things we have to recognize—even as you and I had to recognize because you and I, deep in our hearts, felt that sincere call—is that we recognize the importance of being sent. And who sends us and who discerns that call or that feeling is very, very important. Just because we sense or feel something deeply within us does not necessarily mean that we have this calling to be a priest.

Scott: And you're talking about more than just sincerity. You're talking about conviction. I wouldn't simply have passed the polygraph when I told people I was ordained; I was thoroughly convicted that I was called to minister, that I was ministering. And I *was*. I just wasn't offering the Holy Sacrifice of the Eucharist or hearing Confessions, granting absolution. That precisely is what Christ established Holy Orders for.

Marcus: Let's take this next email: "Dear Marcus and Scott, I recently completed a reading of the Old Testament with the aid of the *Jerome Biblical Commentary*. I was stunned that there was no reference to the practice of baptism per se in the Old Testament. It says John the Baptist's followers were Jews. Where did John get this concept from, and why would Jews be attracted in any significant numbers to follow him out to the desert to get it? Have you been out there in that part of Jerusalem? Since it is not a practice identified in the Torah, where did the word itself come from?"

Scott: Well, that's a good question. I would have to begin by saying that the *Jerome Biblical Commentary* can often help you, but it can often not *entirely* help you. I don't want to criticize it, but I would say it's a mixed bag.

For instance, in the Torah, the five books of Moses, you do have a reference to baptism, as it were, in Numbers 19. It speaks about the purification of ritual impurity or unclean- ness with the water that cleanses. On the third day after getting defiled from some ritual impurity, you had to be sprinkled with this water and then once again on the seventh day. If you look at the Septuagint, the Greek translation of Numbers 19, you'll see it's the only place in the Pentateuch where *baptismal* is used. So, it is baptismal water, not in a New Covenant sacramental sense, but in the shadowy sense of the Old Covenant—cleansing for ritual uncleanness.

Likewise, Ezekiel announces the coming Messiah and the New Covenant and how the Lord will take out the heart of stone and put in the heart of flesh. Then he adds, "For I will take you from the nations, and gather you from all the countries, and bring you into your own land. I will sprinkle clean water upon you, and you shall be clean from all your uncleanness, and from all your idols I will cleanse you. A new heart I will give you, and a new spirit I will put within you" (Ezek. 36:24–26). Notice that the sprinkling of clean water and the cleansing of God's people accompanies the new heart, the new spirit, the New Covenant. It isn't as though John the Baptist were just an innovator or that the Qumran covenanters were just inventing novelties. They had good precedent in the Law and the Prophets for what John the Baptist and Jesus did.

Marcus: Let's go to our next caller, from Illinois. Hello, what's your question for us?

Caller: My question is on Romans 8:28–30: "He also predestined [us] to be conformed to the image of his Son." If He has already predestined us, then why do we need to evangelize?

Scott: That's a good question, but it's not an easy question. The most important thing that you've pointed out is that St. Paul teaches predestination, and St. Paul was a good Catholic. And so the Catholic Church teaches predestination, but it doesn't teach *fatalism*. It doesn't teach that predestination dissolves human freedom or responsibility.

It isn't easy for us to understand how God governs free humans. He gives us intellect, He gives us free will, and He makes us responsible sons and daughters.

Marcus: If we take predestination from the fatalistic standpoint, then why pray? Why do anything in relationship to God, in a sense, if everything is programmed?

Scott: Exactly. We have to say that if God fits the job description for the deity, then He has to know the future, and even more than that, He has created and caused all things. But the way He causes things to happen in human life is He causes them to happen through free wills, freely choosing to obey or disobey. Now, how these two intersect isn't at all easy for us, but we know one thing: that if we advance human freedom at the expense of God's sovereignty, then we end up with a domesticated deity who doesn't fit the job description. But if we advance divine sovereignty as though it dissolves human freedom, we dishonor the very children that God has made in His image and likeness. He's made us free, and yet at the same time, He is sovereign over the future as well as the past and the present. So, He predestines, and we're free.

Marcus: Would you say that in looking back on our Calvinist background, one of the big differences between how we saw it then and how we see things as Catholics is that often as Calvinists or Protestants, everything was either/or, whereas as Catholics, we more appreciate the both/and of mystery?

Scott: I must say, I thought St. Augustine was the solid predestinarian and then St. Thomas Aquinas began to waiver. And then I spent a lot of time—I mean months that actually ended up being years—in Aquinas. Now, I would say the finest treatment in the history of Christian thought of the subject of predestination and freedom, in affirming both equally, is in Aquinas. There's one book I would recommend also. It was recently reprinted, I'm told. It's entitled *Predestination*, and it's written by Fr. Réginald Garrigou-Lagrange. And if you check out either new bookstores or the Internet, you should probably be able to find it. It clarifies and summarizes Augustine, Aquinas, and Paul better than I ever could.

Marcus: I think we have about a minute here. I want to ask you, fourteen years a Catholic now, of all the things that drew you into the Church, if you were to name one thing that made it all worthwhile, looking back on your journey, what was it?

Scott: I had fallen head over heels in love with Jesus as a teenager, and He pulled me out of a big mess that I had made for myself, and then I found Him not just in the Spirit or in my heart, but in the Blessed Sacrament. I mean, I love the pope, the Blessed Mary, the saints, the sacraments, all of it, but to me, the center of it all and the source of it all is Jesus Who is really present in the Holy Eucharist. And that is worth living and dying for.

Marcus: Scott, it is a great privilege. Again, I take this moment to encourage those to look for your new book, *The Lamb's Supper*, which will deal with this issue of the Eucharist and the Mass and help us understand it and appreciate what sometimes we take for granted, and maybe those that are struggling with the Catholic understanding will draw closer.

The Sacramental Basis of Our Hope

Interview with Scott Hahn
(April 2004)

Marcus: Welcome to *The Journey Home*. Our guest tonight is a man who, because of his great love for Jesus and his own conversion to the Church, has had a great influence on many, many others. Many of us are very grateful to Scott Hahn, and it's a privilege to have Scott back.

Scott, if you could remind the audience of your journey into the Church?

Scott: I experienced the grace of conversion as a young teenager around the age of thirteen through Young Life and became a very staunch Evangelical Protestant, dove right into Scripture, fell in love with the Bible, and in high school discerned a call to ministry. It wasn't really a hard decision because I found myself, after a couple of years, so head over heels in love with Our Lord and Scripture, it just seemed to me to be obviously what I was wired for. And at the same time, I was getting a lot of formation that was ... how shall I say? Anti-Catholic.

And so when I wrote my senior paper in high school, it was called "Sola Fide: Luther's Rediscovery of the Gospel," for

Ms. Dangler in English class at the St. Clare High School. So, I was really targeting my Catholic friends and that sort of thing. I went through Young Life for four years as a college student, triple major in theology, philosophy, and economics. I wanted to repay the debt of gratitude to Our Lord by working to reach unchurched kids like I had been reached, and I also targeted the Catholic kids because I considered them sort of unreached. Since then, I've sent care packages to all of the Catholic kids I tried to get out of the Church, just to reinforce their faith. But the long and the short of it is, after graduating in 1979 from college and getting married to the most beautiful gal on campus, Kimberly and I moved up to Boston. We began a three-year program, and I started getting a master's in theology, with you, at Gordon-Conwell Seminary. I remember I really helped you get through school. I taught you everything I knew in basketball, and that took about four hours. We had a lot of fun. It was our first couple of years, and Kimberly began to rethink the issue of artificial birth control—contraception—and it opened my eyes and then my heart, and we changed. I think that, in a certain way, opened us up to even more light, to more truth.

By the time I was graduating in '82, I went on to pastor a small church in Fairfax, Virginia—Trinity Presbyterian. And the result of studying Scripture, studying the early Church Fathers, going deeper and deeper—I was really disturbed because everything kept coming up Catholic, and that was especially hard for me because I had been so anti-Catholic. Then pastoring a church, I was disturbed how pastor-centered the church was, how sermon-centered the services were each Sunday, and so I really urged them, instead of celebrating the Lord's Supper, as we called it, four times a year, I suggested that we follow Calvin's advice and do it every week. Eventually, the elders agreed, and we did it, and it really had a great influence on our own sense of solidarity and fellowship. But it also had a great influence on me because the more I studied, the more I saw that while there is liturgy at every point in Scripture throughout salvation history, there was hardly any liturgy in my own personal spiritual experience. And so after about a year and a half or so, I had studied and prayed myself into a crisis of faith, resigned, spent about two years studying intensely, and then moved to Milwaukee in 1985 to begin a doctoral program in biblical theology.

Thinking I would wait at least five years until 1990 at the earliest, I fell in with the wrong crowd. That was a congregation of believers at a midday Mass in a basement chapel, and all of my study and all of my prayer and all of my research, and all of my resolution not to become Catholic, it just ... when I heard a Roman Catholic priest pronounce the words of consecration for the first time in my life, I felt like doubting Thomas. I remember feeling like the last drops of doubt were draining out of my brain, out of my heart, and I was whispering, "My Lord, my God, that's You. I know that's You."

At that point, everything sped up, and within a matter of weeks, I had spoken to Msgr. Bruskewitz, who is now the bishop out in Lincoln, Nebraska; he had given me approval to be received in the Church. And it was hard for Kimberly, who didn't come in until, ironically, 1990, but the experience was just overwhelming. It was such a sense of homecoming. At the same time, there was such a sense of loneliness, because I didn't really know how to share this with my Protestant brothers and sisters who really had no interest, and it was hard to relate at times to the cradle Catholics who kind of looked and smiled and nodded and said, "That's nice." But over a period of three or four years, I realized that I had been prepared for this, in my biblical training, in all the other theological, philosophical formation. In fact, I am more grateful now for my Evangelical formation than I ever was when I was an Evangelical pastor. I just see how the Lord brought so many convergent influences into my life to prepare me for what He obviously wanted me to do.

Marcus: I know you've mentioned this before, and when you summarize your journey in many ways, it sounds very cognitive—you've worked through all those issues—but you mentioned that you found this very on-fire little congregation. Could you talk to the audience a bit about the importance of the Catholic witness, the Catholic layperson who modeled the Faith for you during that time when you were still struggling on your journey? As you were beginning to understand, what difference did it make, seeing it fleshed out?

Scott: For me, growing up, I had never seen it fleshed out. I had a lot of good Catholic friends, but they were the only ones who could outdrink me, and so I didn't really look upon them as the paragon of devotion. And when I left the pastorate, I was hard-pressed to find Catholics who were really devout. When I got to Marquette, I found some priests and fellow graduate students and others who lived it out with a great sense of excitement and gratitude but also with a certain naturalness. The greatness that I saw about the Catholic Faith was not simply the theology students or the priests, but it was the housewives, the businessmen who would skip a lunch hour to come in for daily Mass, and just the ordinary person. I realized, this is a Faith that is for the priests and the scholars and the peasants, and the bag ladies who would come in off the side streets and the alleys in downtown Milwaukee. I saw real devotion — not much theological depth — but I realized, if this is a family and not just a health spa for an all-star team, then God the Father loves those peasants, and the bag ladies, as much as the grad students. And boy, what a sense of universal family and homecoming it was — even before I was officially received.

And so, as I got to know Catholics better, and I saw the way that they lived a little more quietly perhaps, I realized that still waters run deep, as they say. You might see a couple out in a restaurant, wining and dining, and he's got a rose, he's got chocolate, and they're talking and staring into each other's eyes, but then on the other side of the restaurant, you might see a couple who've been married for forty years, and they hardly exchange twenty words. They look into each other's eyes with deep mutual understanding, they've raised their kids, they've sacrificed for each other. Where is the love? We automatically associate it with the intensity, the enthusiasm, the passion. But in Catholics, I really came to see ... And I want to say to the cradle Catholics: "Thanks for holding down the fort." But even more: "Thanks for loving in those quiet, deep ways and living out the zeal year after year, not necessarily in a flashy or noisy way, but just with consistency."

Marcus: You also mentioned a little bit ago about how thankful you are for your Evangelical roots, which I am too. I've always told the guests on this program that this program is not an anti-Protestant program, because we found Jesus through the witness of these men and women, or professors or pastors, and we are eternally grateful to them. But you also mentioned that there's a fulfillment aspect of your Evangelicalism. I want to ask you to comment on something, which to some people is a controversial statement from Vatican II, but I think it's very important. In fact, I first learned it in Fr. Hardon's catechism, when he says that whatever the Holy Spirit has engraved in the hearts of our separated brethren is for *our* spiritual renewal. I was thinking you could talk a bit about that because that's a really positive statement that connects us.

Scott: I'd love to. I'd like to do it, though, by backing up an extra step or two, because tonight's the night the Jews celebrate Passover. I remember studying Passover for the first time as a Protestant pastor in order to incorporate all of that into an explanation of Holy Week, because that's what Holy Week was all about for Jesus and the disciples and everybody else in Jerusalem. You have the full flowering of Judaism, the Lamb of God Who takes away the sins of the world, the Firstborn Who dies. You have the new Passover in Christ Who is the Lamb of God, and until you really grasp the Jewish roots of the Christian faith, you can't appreciate Jesus, much less the Eucharist. And so, studying that made me more deeply appreciative of Who Jesus was and what He did, as Christianity is the full flowering of Judaism. Pope Pius XI said that, spiritually speaking, we're all Semites. You can't be a good Catholic and not love the Jewish religion and the roots of our Faith. So as a Protestant, I looked at the Passover and said this makes so much more sense out of Holy Week and Good Friday and the Resurrection and everything else. But then I went from Jesus being a Lamb to the Eucharist, and I'm like, *wow*, you know, if Christianity is the full flowering of Judaism, then Catholicism is the full flowering and the highest expression of biblical Christianity.

We share so much more in common with Protestants than what we differ on, and I think it's always important to build on that common ground—not to ignore the differences, because they're significant, but not to bypass the common ground, which is so much more substantial. The Trinity and the Bible and our prayers and so much more. Baptism itself. I just think that we've got to engage in these kinds of conversations with separated brothers and sisters, not to win arguments, but to show them where they can find the Jesus they love and serve, sometimes more generously than we do. And I think that is really why, for me, the Holy Eucharist is the source and the summit of my faith as a Catholic Christian now.

Marcus: Well, I know you've written a lot about that, Scott. Your book on the sacraments is one book I really appreciate—*Lord, Have Mercy: The Healing Power of Confession*, which refers back to your previous book *The Lamb's Supper*. And you have a new book coming out?

Scott: Yes, *Swear to God: The Promise and Power of the Sacraments*, and I have to tell you, it is by far and away my favorite—it's the one I think I've worked longer and harder at and tried to simplify so that Catholics can realize what I discovered about eighteen years ago. Sacraments aren't mere ritual, they're not the things that we do for God. They are the things that God does for us. And man alive, are they rooted in Scripture, especially when you read the New and the Old Testaments together the way the early Church did.

Marcus: We do have a call already and also an email. Let's go with the email. This one comes from Minnesota: "Dr. Hahn, your name came up with my Lutheran pastor friend who told me he was scared to read your conversion story. What can you tell him that would open his heart to pick up your books?"

Scott: Well, I wouldn't tell him to pick up my books, I would just tell him to be sure to embrace the Light and not to sin against that. Because you know what the Light is, you know Who the Light is, that is Jesus Christ. And whenever He called me into painful and uncomfortable discoveries, it was always worth it. As my wife likes to say, "The Lord will never be outdone in generosity." And so, I would say it to him, to anybody, if you get an interior sense that God wants to show you more of His love, and He wants to show it to you in places you might not have seen it before, don't turn away, don't value anything more than those gifts that come from God.

Marcus: We don't want him to accept it because you said it or I said or someone else said it—we want him to accept it because it's true. We don't want him to be afraid of what's true, because it's of God. So, he shouldn't be in any way afraid of what's true.

Scott: And as a Lutheran, he knows that Jesus Christ is the source and the summit of our life. He knows that in the Bible we have the Word inspired; he knows that there is more truth to be discovered for himself and for his people.

And so if the Holy Spirit speaks to you through this particular writing or that particular speaker, just be sure to embrace the Light, welcome the Truth, don't sin against whatever light God gives you.

Marcus: And you keep praying for your friend; don't you dare stop praying for him.

Scott: And keep deepening the friendship.

Marcus: Exactly, that's how evangelization works: through friendships. Let's take our first caller. This is from Michigan. Hello. What's your question for us?

Caller: Marcus and Scott, thank you so much. You showed me how to get home. Will you share how your journeys impacted your own personal relationships with your own fathers?

Scott: My dad was an agnostic almost all of his life. His mother, my grandmother, was a devout Catholic, but married outside the Church and kind of drifted away, and then after her husband died — my grandfather — she rediscovered her faith and then some, with a deep, quiet, but devout integrity. And so when I grew up, all I remembered were the rosary beads and these other kinds of things. And when I first became a Catholic, other family members were not so happy at all. My dad took me aside and said — and this is the agnostic father who was brilliant, who was virtuous and upright — he said, "I know one thing. Your grandmother would be proud." And then he said, "And so am I." And this is painful, but within about two years, he contracted an illness that became the disease that took his life in 1991, and I watched him suffer for a year, and it was some of the hardest experience I ever went through, but I also learned that the theology of redemptive suffering is practical and powerful, and it can reach into the minds of brilliant agnostics, and it can touch the hearts of fathers, like mine, who are suffering.

I remember walking into his hospital room, and he hadn't shaved. I never saw him like that. And I offered to shave him—it's my dad, he changed my diapers, the least I can do is shave him, so I did, and then I asked him if I could read the Bible. He said, "Yeah, I'd like that." And so, I thought I was kind of forcing it, but then I started reading, and I thought he was asleep, and I stopped, and he opened his eyes and said, "Keep reading, this is really good." So, I read until he fell asleep, and I came back several more times, and we talked about prayer, we talked about God, we talked about how through suffering, through humiliation, he was being made more like a little child. And in the last few weeks of his life, I saw my father—I wish I could say he entered the Church and received the sacraments—but I will say, what graces he received were all a prelude. Without going into any detail, I just have to thank my heavenly Father for the gift of my earthly father, praying for the repose of his soul, but I also want to thank God for the grace He gave to him in the last weeks of his life. I was the only one there at his bedside when he breathed his last. I closed his eyes, I dropped to my knees, and for the first time in my life, I had no other father but God. And I just said, "God, please receive my father, and make him a little brother, and thank You—*thank You*—for him." And that's about all I can say. Thank you for the question.

Marcus: I'm not going to go into it all about my father, but it's amazing how parallel our experiences were. My dad was a similar agnostic, or at least not talking about his faith for so long. And really, it was through my own conversion to the Church—same thing—his comment was, "Well, if I were to become active in a Christian church, it would be the Catholic Church." So, he was open to it, and it's a long, long story, very similar to yours, but he was the reason that I did *The Journey Home* program. He was the reason that I wrote *How Firm a Foundation*, because I wanted to reach him. You know that old thing about a prophet in his own town and how hard it is to reach your parents or siblings? But just in the end, slowly and slowly, through your witness and others in *The Journey Home*, week after week — until on the last day, which turned out to be his last day of life, finally a priest visited him in the hospital, prayed with him, and so I felt quite confident that comfort was there for him in the end. And since I mentioned him every week, I know that some of you were praying there at home for him because I let you know what he was going through. I appreciate that so much.

And in many ways, I credit my wife, Marilyn, more than anything, because she gave him the rosary beads, taught him how to pray the Rosary, and he revealed to me that he would say the Our Father and use the rosary beads — as emphysema was making it so hard for him to breathe — he would use the Our Father to get back into control.

Let's take this next email. This one comes in from Elmira, New York: "Evangelicals present an attractive proposition when they say you can know for sure that if you died tonight you would go to Heaven. Doesn't a baptized Catholic who truly repents and confesses and relies on Jesus' sacrifice on the Cross have a similar assurance? Most Catholics would say, 'Well, I hope so.' To the Evangelical, that sounds as if the Catholic does not know the basis for salvation, or as if even his Confession made in good faith might not be enough to save him. How can Catholics express confidence in the sufficiency of Christ's sacrifice in a more positive way?"

Scott: Wow, this is a great question. And she used the keyword *assurance* because assurance is the biblical term. It's the Church's term. We talk a lot about the three theological virtues—faith, hope, and love—but actually, we talk a lot more about faith and love than we do hope. It's the assurance of hope, that's what the writer of Hebrews talks about in chapters 11 and 12. But already back in Hebrews 6, he explains how faith is rooted in the Word of God: whatever God promises, you must believe. In Hebrews 6:13 and following, besides the word of promise, God adds an oath, and that is the basis for the assurance of hope. Now, when we hear that, it sounds legalistic, it sounds juridical, but this is where my new book comes in, *Swear to God: The Promise and Power of the Sacraments*, because every liturgy consists of word and sacrament; every liturgy gives a promise of God and then an oath, a *sacramentum*, because *sacramentum* is the Latin word for oath. And I would say that if you look at the Word of God, you see the basis for faith, but it's when you go into the sacraments that you see that Catholics don't have lesser grounds for the assurance of hope—we have far greater grounds.

Now, a lot of Protestants say, "Oh, it isn't assurance. It's certainty. Once saved, always saved." But I like what a friend of mine, Mike Forester, who has written a two-volume book as a Protestant, says: "Once saved, always saved, *if you don't fall away*." That's the big *if*. And this is what so many of our fellow Protestants really bypass or ignore, because the fact is you have to persevere.

So, there is the authentic assurance that the sacraments give us. And there can be a false certainty that people boast about which they don't necessarily possess. "On that day many will say to me, 'Lord, Lord,' ... And then will I declare to them, 'I never knew you; depart from me'" (Matt. 7:22–23).

140

Marcus: A lot of our Protestant brothers and sisters make a big thing out of the book of Revelation—they really run with Revelation. But talk a bit about the seven churches. To each of the seven churches, Jesus says, "To him who conquers ..." It's in there every time, this need to persevere.

Scott: In Revelation 2 and 3, you have the seven letters to the seven churches in Asia Minor. Eight times, Jesus says, "Repent, repent, repent. Or else I'll come and remove your lampstand." And then He adds, "But he who conquers, he'll get the Tree of Life. He who conquers will get a new name. He who conquers will enter the New Jerusalem." And so, God has given to us the means, the basis for firm faith, for firm hope, and for this firm and deep and growing charity, for love. But this idea of hope, this is the neglected virtue, and I've got to tell you, Catholics really do need to lay hold of the sacramental basis for the assurance of hope. It's not like "I hope I win the lottery," or "I hope our team wins the Super Bowl." It's more like "I hope I get down to Birmingham today." I had a good travel agent; I got a ticket, pretty good airlines, and I got a ride to the airport; I've done this before. I had firm assurance that I would be here. Well, we've got firmer assurance because we've got God giving us His Word, and then adding an oath and receiving these sacraments give us that assurance.

Marcus: You pointed out so well, Scott, one reason that maybe we don't have this hope is that the devil has reengineered the meaning of the words *faith, hope,* and *love* by the way they've been belittled and abused and overused in our culture to the point where they lose the power of what it really means when we talk about theological faith, theological hope, and theological love. We need to recapture that so we can teach it to our children.

Let's take our next call, from Texas. What's your question for us?

Caller: I used to be a Mormon missionary and a leader in the Mormon Church, and I'm a convert to Catholicism for less than two years. How do I answer my Mormon friends, those that are still my friends, who say that the Catholic Church lost its apostolic authority in the Dark Ages, and that's what required God to come back and give the gospel to Joseph Smith?

Scott: Sometimes they trace it back to even before the medieval period, all the way to the second and third centuries. So the great "apostasy" occurred at various points, according to various proponents of this theory. I would say the bottom line is: Can we take God at His Word or not? Can we trust Jesus when He makes a statement like this: "On this rock I will build my church" (Matt. 16:18)? He didn't say, "Peter, go build Me a church, and James and John, while you're at it, you build Me one too." He said, "On this rock I will build my church." Now, we know that Peter as a rock could be a stumbling stone, because five verses later that's what Jesus calls him. But when Jesus says, "On this rock I will build my church," you know that Peter is not the builder, he is the tool. Jesus is the builder, and He's the owner of the Church. And so, when Jesus adds, "And the gates of Hades shall not prevail against this Church that I build, because it's My Church," you can be sure that when God the Father sends the Son with all authority in Heaven and earth and imparts the Spirit to men who would be otherwise fallible, He can impart to them the infallibility that they need to get the word out, to get the gospel across, to get the nations to hear the whole truth and nothing but the truth because they've got God's help. And so, I would say, look at the Word of God, listen to the words of Jesus, and look at how He began with a guy like Peter and how He sustained it through Linus, Cletus, Clement, Sixtus, and all the others—the 250-some popes who have gone all the way back.

Marcus: I was even thinking that there's the misnomer of the "Dark Ages." It just illustrates the ignorance of history. Really, it just blankets these years as dark and ignorant, as if there were no writings during that time.

Scott: It is a mythical conception. It reminds me of that book, *The Myth of the Flat Earth*. You cannot find any point in the Middle Ages where men believed that the earth was flat. That was a nineteenth-century invention to make it look that the more Christian a civilization was, the darker it was, and so the Enlightenment had to kind of restore reason. It's just unholy hogwash. I would say, at the same time, that there *were* bad popes, like Sylvester and Honorius, and others too, but the fact is, Jesus began with a guy like Peter to show us that it's the work of Christ. It's not the work of Pope John Paul II or John Paul I or Paul VI. I don't think John Paul II wants us to put our trust in *him* but in Christ, and the Holy Spirit is capable of working through him. And so, when you study the medieval period, you see some really great popes, you see some mediocre popes, you see a few bad ones, but you see an unbroken spiritual dynasty, the likes of which history has never seen before, and it's not because the Vatican's so special or these guys were so well educated. It's because Jesus Christ is faithful and all-powerful.

Marcus: I would recommend a used book, and you have to search for this one, and maybe Scott can think of one too, but I found this in a used bookstore. It's out of print, but it's called *Pageant of the Popes*. It's very readable, it goes through all the stories of the popes, and it doesn't pull any punches, but it's a wonderful story of their lives, and it just helps you see this continuity that's there. I don't know if there's another book you'd recommend, Scott?

Scott: That would be a good one. There are a lot of others. I'm thinking of Archbishop Miller, who has a great book, *The Shepherd and the Rock*, about Peter and the papacy. But I'm thinking, too, when I was a Protestant, I looked at the 250-some popes they had, and there were some really bad ones, and I can still see that as a Catholic. But you can count them and keep it in the single digits. And that's the truth for Protestants too; even when I was an anti-Catholic, I had to admit there weren't as many bad ones as I expected. When you look at the Davidic dynasty, from David through Solomon, Hezekiah, and Josiah, all the way to the Babylon captivity, something like 80 percent of them were rotten to the core. And yet God was not ashamed to identify Himself with that line, to bind Himself by a covenant oath to produce His own Son in that line, to fulfill that covenant. So, if God can do it in the Davidic dynasty, then how much more can Christ establish it through the spiritual line!

Marcus: Excellent point. To our next caller, from Delaware.

Caller: Hi, Marcus, thank you so much for taking my question. My husband and I watch your program every Monday, Marcus, and I met both of you last summer at the Defending the Faith conference in Steubenville, which was wonderful. Well, first of all, I was raised Catholic; I left the Church sixteen years ago and have been in a PCA Presbyterian Church, which I think is your background, Scott. I've been at it for sixteen years, and I am coming back to the Catholic Church in May. I've read your books and many other books, but my question is: When you left the Protestant church, how long did it take you to feel Catholic and to find your place?

Scott: Hmm, let me see ... Well, in a certain sense, I still feel like a convert. I was at the Pittsburgh airport this morning, and as I was coming up the escalator to go to my gate, I'm like, "Oh, Lord, what I wouldn't do for the Sacrament." Suddenly, over the PA: "Catholic Mass will be held in ten minutes in the chapel," and I'm like, "Oh, yeah!" And so, I went up there, and afterward I was with Fr. Fitzgerald for a few minutes, and he took me out for coffee. But it dawned on me, I'm Catholic eighteen years, but it doesn't feel all that different than it was after eighteen months. So, in a certain sense, I still feel newborn, I still feel the zeal of a convert.

But I think you're asking a deeper question, and that is one that involves inculturation, because as a convert of eighteen years, I think I'm losing a little bit of my Evangelical dialect. I still sound a little Protestant, but Thomas Aquinas and the liturgy and all of these other saints and Fathers have shaped my thought and my outlook on life and my own family experience as well. But I would say that the grace of conversion is ongoing for me, and so I'm always feeling like I've got more to go. I've come so far, but I also want to use it as an occasion to say this: every Catholic is a convert, once we understand conversion. Because as the Holy Father says, it's the grace of ongoing and ever-deepening conversion.

And so the grace of conversion is going to be alive and fruitful for you and for so many other people this Easter within the next week or so. But yeah, it was hard for a Presbyterian, who had been anti-Catholic, to feel at home. But my love for Scripture, my conviction that it's true, and then the conclusion that it all comes up Catholic—whether the emotions are there or not—I knew I was home, and I knew that I knew that I knew.

Marcus: It's that old image of the pilgrim in *Pilgrim's Progress*, with the bag full of rocks and stuff: it takes a while even after you come into the Church. I used to use the image that you could move to France and probably take a test after a while and become a Frenchman, but it would take a long time for the other natural-born Frenchman to mistake you for a real Frenchman. Just think of all the barriers because of language and culture and all of this. The same is true for those of us that have been Protestant all our lives. But the other issue is really learning the true meaning of some of the stuff that we do as Catholics.

Scott: I just thought of something while you were talking—another advantage that we both were given is the study of Scripture at Gordon-Conwell. Places like that really teach you to trust God's Word, to want more of it, to study it whenever you can, to preach it, to teach it, to share it, and to meditate upon that sort of thing. To have biblical literacy carries you a long way into the Catholic Church because the Mass is just saturated with Scripture.

A couple of years ago, my wife and I started the St. Paul Center for Biblical Theology, because we had noticed in becoming Catholic how many Catholics didn't have biblical literacy, and in fact, I've even found some clergy who didn't really know the Bible all that well. And so, it dawned on me one day that the Mass is the only thing that every Catholic has to go to, all around the world, every week; and the Bible is the only thing that has to be read in the Mass every week for every Catholic. And it's always the Old and the New Testaments read together; it's always the promises of the Old and their fulfillment by Christ in the New Testament. So, biblical literacy for Catholics is something that we are just absolutely determined to establish, to impart biblical fluency for the clergy, for the teachers, this sort of thing. Because when you read the Bible, you hear God's Word; but when you read the Bible from the heart of the Church—that's the motto and the mission of the St. Paul Center—it's in the liturgy, it's always the Old in the New. You don't just preach on your favorite verse the way we sometimes did; you always hear the Old and the New, and you preach, and you pray the Scriptures that take you all the way through salvation history, from Genesis to Jesus, through the book of Revelation. Catholics get more of the Bible in the Mass than any Protestant churches you will go to.

Marcus: Sometimes I think that, even though Catholics hear the Scriptures read more often than we did, part of the reason that it doesn't always connect for them is because the lectionary is broken up here and there, all over the place; we hear it on Sunday, but often we're not encouraged to take the Bible and read it beginning to end, so that, when we hear it on Sunday, we can put it together and see how it fits into the story.

Scott: That's true, that's really true. But what we *do* hear is significant. I remember working on Peter and the papacy in Matthew 16 and finding the keys in Isaiah 22 and thinking, "Man, am I clever! Is this original!" I wrote a graduate paper for a doctoral seminar, and I think I blew most of the seminar away. I know the Lutheran professor was surprised to see it. I was so proud of myself. About three weeks later, I go to Mass on a weekday, and the reading from the Old Testament is Isaiah 22, the exact same verses, and then the Gospel reading is Matthew 16—Peter and the keys! I'm thinking, "What is this, the lectionary lottery?" Then I looked, and every year, those texts are read. I think Catholics are a lot like kids who grew up in a neighborhood, who know it really well, but they don't know the street addresses like the mailman might, and then when I finally got my learner's permit, I began to connect this neighborhood with that street, and this with that street, and that's what we want to impart to Catholics.

Marcus: Let's take our next caller, from Michigan.

Caller: My question is, what was it about Church teaching that changed your views on contraception even before you joined the Church?

Scott: Good question. This is the climax of the book *Swear to God*. I spend three chapters on sex, lies, and sacraments, and it was an exciting and a scary discovery because I was so convinced that the Bible is the key to understanding Jesus. And if the covenant is the key to understanding the Bible, and I just entered into a covenant called marriage right before we began a serious graduate study for ministry ... Well, the first year of our marriage, Kimberly comes to me, and she's studying this issue, and she hands me a book, *Birth Control and the Marriage Covenant*, and it's by a Catholic, John Kippley. I'm like: "I thought I owned every book with the word *covenant* in the title! But what's a Catholic doing writing a book about covenant and then tying it to birth control?" Well, I began to read it, and I realized that every covenant is sealed by a kind of ritual act, like animal sacrifice. Marriage is a covenant ratified by the marital act, sexual intimacy, when the spouses are united. And what he shows is that when covenants are ratified and renewed, they release grace. When the marriage covenant is ratified and then renewed, it releases a very special grace, it releases life, it reveals God's own life-giving love.

It dawned on me, as I was reading through this book, that when God made man, it says the two become one, and the one they become is so real that nine months later you end up giving it a name. And I thought: "This is so mysterious. It's so powerful." And then I began to read the Bible, and I even read Luther and Calvin and the Protestants, and they all agreed with the Catholic Church's teaching. When I finally got around to reading *Humanae Vitae*, Kimberly and I prayed about it, we talked about it, and we threw away our contraception, and shortly thereafter, the two became one, and three, with Michael conceived twenty-one years ago.

Marcus: How many children now?

Scott: I got six kids from twenty-one down to four.

Marcus: Wow, praise God. Praise God, really.

It looks like we have an email: "Hello from Guam, USA, where America's day begins, where I'm trying to watch on the Internet due to the special program. First, let me express my deepest thanks to both of you, Marcus and Scott, for all you've done to help me grow in faith. I'm a cradle Catholic who took my Catholicism for granted until a friend who was once a Catholic but is now a Christian invited me to leave the Church and join her in her walk with the Lord. That's when, by the grace of God, I discovered EWTN and both of you. Anyway, I have a couple of questions for Scott. In your conversion story, you mentioned that prior to becoming a Catholic, you had worked hard to get Catholics to leave the Church. I understand this was all done in good faith, and I imagine you were quite successful in your efforts. Since your conversion to Catholicism, have you been able to contact, or have you heard from any of those people? Have you been able to convince any of them to return to the Church? Gentleman, keep up the awesome work. God bless you."

Scott: I think I have tracked down each and every one of them over the years, and I have sent free books and free tapes. And with two possible exceptions—I lost touch with two of them—but the others have come back into the Church. And that's really the grace of God. It's not anything to do with me, but it's really a special thing; it's a fun, joyful kind of thing; it's like restitution.

Marcus: I haven't been quite so successful, and part of the reason is that in the congregations where I pastored, I would say at least 30 or 40 percent of each church were ex-Catholics, and the rest, they were just ex-everybody else. So, I don't know if I ever converted anybody from nothing; they were ex-Episcopalians, ex-whatever, and they were finding Jesus, we were bringing them into the church without apologies—hey, if they're not going to feed them, well, then I'm going to feed them. So, I look back, and I'm a little embarrassed at how flippant I was about that, about just going out and bringing them into the church.

Scott: Sheep-stealing, in a certain sense, no matter what you want to call it.

Marcus: We had this form, we just filled it out, sent a copy to the other pastor, just to let you know they're no longer a member of your church, they're now a member of mine. I don't know if it was the case for you, Scott, but so many of those Catholics, once they "found Jesus," a part of their conversion was to be so thankful they were freed from the "whore of Babylon," and I just confirmed all that.

Scott: And the answer is not to get argumentative or angry or reactionary, the answer is to go deeper into Scripture to receive more grace from the sacraments. We have, I've mentioned, the St. Paul Center for Biblical Theology, with a website where we've put just literally thousands of pages of free instruction for Scripture, for apologetics, about Mary, the pope, Purgatory, the saints. All the tapes I have done over the years are available, all of the books as well, because we want to equip Catholics not to feel defensive, not to feel argumentative, but to really say, "Look, when we're discussing Scripture, that's a home game; that's not an away game." And when we gather together to study Scripture or we gather together to celebrate the Mass, it isn't just the Word of God inspired, it's the Word of God incarnate, it's really Jesus there.

Marcus: I love that verse which you and I both refer to a lot in 1 Peter — "Always be prepared to make a defense ... for the hope that is in you" (1 Pet. 3:15) — and it's interesting, it draws us back to that virtue of hope. That's what all this is about, giving us the assurance of that hope, so that we can then share it with others, so they can experience that hope, and that's what we want for our separated brethren, to just have true hope and their faith based on a firm foundation.

Scott: But we have to underscore the fact that it isn't emotion, it isn't just feeling, it isn't just kind of sitting around and waiting for God to zap you. You have to pray. But you also have to study; you have to read. And right now, we have witnessed, since becoming Catholics, a renaissance in Catholic literature.

When we started www.salvationhistory.com as a website, we wanted to go out and pull together all of the Bible study resources, and then we discovered you can't keep track. We spent another six months, and we got more. We put some online courses up, and then we found some more. The amount of Bible study apologetics resources that are online — it's astounding — and the number of people who are going online finding it, reading it, is just growing by leaps and bounds.

Marcus: Let's take another email: "Hi, Marcus and Dr. Hahn. You both are great sons of the Church, and I draw inspiration from you both. My question is this: What do I say to family members who are convinced that Easter is a pagan holiday? They say that the name *Easter* can't be found in the Bible. So, what do you say?"

Scott: I would say, "Jesus is risen; He is risen indeed." The New England Puritans outlawed the celebration of Easter, and certain Protestant denominations did that for many centuries. It wasn't really until the 1800s that Protestants became more and more comfortable with Christmas and Easter and that sort of thing, but the plain fact is that it *is* in the New Testament. The celebration of Easter is what the gospel is all built up to, and so for us to go through the life of Jesus, for us to study the Old Testament background, for us to read what Paul has to say about Christ, but to ignore the fact that the Resurrection changed the world ... Well, why would you celebrate your birthday but not the Resurrection? Why would you celebrate your anniversary and not the Resurrection? This is what ushered in a whole new creation, this is what guarantees our salvation.

Marcus: The issue in the early days of the Church was not whether to celebrate Easter; it was *when*.

Scott: That's right. The debate was how to calculate it with respect to the Jewish Passover, the lunar cycle, the full moon, the spring equinox, and all of the rest. But again, you're not out to win arguments. You want to listen to that person, find common ground, and answer the best you can in a spirit of friendship.

Marcus: Let's take this next email: "Is it true that Marcus and Scott attended a Protestant seminary in a building that formally housed a monastery?"

That is true. The main difference was that Scott always hid out in the old confessional, studying, and I was in the infirmary, playing basketball.

Scott: I played racquetball ball there too. But yes, Gordon-Conwell Seminary was a Carmelite monastery. They ended up taking down all the statues, but not before the Carmelites went through the formal official process of desacralizing the monastery.

Marcus: The altar was still there when we were there.

Scott: That's right, but they took out the relics and all of the things that had to be removed. I remember running into Fr. Kilian Healy, a Carmelite who was there for many, many years, and he said, "I used to teach there," and I'm like, "No, it's an Evangelical Protestant seminary." He said, "You don't understand, young man. It was Carmelite until we sold it in 1970." And then he looked at me and said, "You know, we give them the seminary, they give us the graduates. That seems like a pretty fair deal to me." It was a great, great time.

Marcus: This next email comes from Watervliet, New York: "Dear Marcus and Dr. Scott, I am hoping you will receive this email in time. Dr. Scott, thank you so much for your witness in the Catholic Faith. Have either of you explored the Maronite or other Eastern Catholic Rites, and what were your impressions? Thank you, Marcus, for an awesome program. I never miss *The Journey Home* and have referred many Protestants who are seeking answers regarding Catholicism to the Coming Home Network."

Scott: I read the Latin Fathers of the West, the Greek Fathers in the East, but I love the Syriac tradition. And that's really what the Maronite Rite is based upon. And to be honest, I was seriously considering going Byzantine Catholic, because the first liturgy I went to wasn't a Mass; it was a Byzantine Catholic Vespers at Sts. Cyril and Methodius Seminary in Pittsburgh. When I walked out after all the incense and prostrations I had witnessed, I thought: "Now I know why I've got a body!" I still to this day just soak in the Maronite Rite materials, the Syriac tradition, as well as the Byzantine and Eastern Catholic tradition.

Marcus: I read a book every morning, page by page, as a part of my morning devotions. It's called the *Philokalia*. I love that and strongly encourage it. I just have the first volume of it, but I have never found a clearer description of the mystical theology of the heart and the need to protect and guard the heart, and the beauty of that and also the need for the fear of the Lord as a part of our journey of faith. I find that more clearly expressed in the Eastern Fathers often. We lost it a little bit in the West, it seems, but I'm with John Paul II that we've got to have both sides.

Scott: Breathe with both lungs. *The Lamb's Supper* was actually based upon a lot of the Eastern Catholic tradition about the Mass being Heaven on earth, going through the book of Revelation and showing how the liturgy of Heaven is what you find on every single page of the Apocalypse.

Marcus: Scott, how about drawing it to a close by talking about how your journey into the Catholic Church deepened your faith in Christ, which you already had for many years.

Scott: I remember my father-in-law giving a sermon on John 7:37–38: "If any one thirst, let him come to me and drink.... 'Out of his heart shall flow rivers of living water.'"

He challenged us when I was still a Protestant. He said, "You know how hard we work for just a little trickle." And I remember asking Our Lord, "Pour out living waters." And I tell you, when I began to discover the sacraments, that's where I found the Holy Spirit just gushing forth in living water. I always loved Jesus, I always took God at His Word, but when you come to the Church, and you find Christ in the Eucharist and all seven sacraments—you know, I was talking to Kimberly several months ago about how to get this excitement across to Catholics, how to get them into the Bible.

Marcus: Scott, thank you for joining us again on *The Journey Home*. It's always a great pleasure.

Reading Scripture as a Catholic Christian
Interview with Scott Hahn
(August 2008)

Marcus: Welcome to *The Journey Home*. We've got a special guest this evening. He's special for lots of reasons. You've seen Dr. Scott Hahn in many programs and you've probably read his books, or I hope you have, but he's also special because he's a classmate of mine from seminary, and sometimes I'm still amazed at that.

Scott, I remember the enthusiasm and zeal and fervency that you had for Calvin and Calvinism, even more than I did.

Scott: More than most people in the seminary.

Marcus: Yes, that's another story, but it's also good to see that same deep commitment and zeal and fervor still, and your love for the Catholic Church. And that's what we're here to talk about.

In fact, I would just mention that thirty years ago is when I began seminary. Thirty years ago, you were just about ready. You know what, it's funny—this is completely off-topic—Gordon-Conwell wasn't my first choice. It was between Princeton and Gordon-Conwell, and I tried to decide.

Scott: You chose wisely.

Marcus: I chose Gordon-Conwell because it was the Young Life school, because I thought I was going to be in Young Life. Was that your first choice, Gordon-Conwell?

Scott: It was. I had a couple of other choices, but when professors were shuffled around, it became pretty clear I wanted to study under M. G. Kline and Roger Nicole. The lineup there was very impressive.

Marcus: That just shows the difference. You were doing the intelligent thing, the professors. I made sure they had racquetball courts and a basketball court, that's what I was looking for with the seminary.

Well, on every *Journey Home* program in this open-line format, I invite the returning guests to give a little five-minute or so summary of their story on what brought them into the Church.

Scott: It's the year of St. Paul, what an amazing time to be together, because here is the great example, the model convert, perhaps the most thoroughly converted man in Christian history. As I was reflecting on his life the last few weeks after the year began in late June, I began to notice some parallels between his life and mine.

He was raised as a Roman citizen, the foremost power of his day, and he was cultured and well educated so that in his early teens—they were in Tarsus—he made a decision to go and study under arguably the greatest theologian of that century, Rabban Gamaliel. Most of them were called rabbis, but he was the first rabbi that they called *rabban*, which means "our teacher." There was a saying among the rabbis that when Gamaliel died, the glory of the Torah perished. And so as a teenager or in his early twenties, Paul went to study under Gamaliel, and I look back in my own life because I was converted to Christ through Young Life in my mid-teens, and then for the next several years, I pursued Scripture with this holy fervor. I went to Grove City College and I went to Gordon-Conwell Seminary because I saw that these had the men who were going to make the Scripture come alive. So, I had my own Gamaliels. And just as Saul the Pharisee, who had graduated as a prized pupil under this great, great professor, came to a sudden decisive turning point in his own life in his mid-to-late twenties, so did I, after graduating top of my class as an Evangelical Christian with strong anti-Catholic convictions.

My love for Scripture was always greater than my contempt for Catholic ritualism and superstition, so I found in the Fathers more connections between the Old and the New, and in their homilies they made the Bible come alive. I kept absorbing more and more, going deeper and deeper, and discovering that Baptism is a lot more than I realized, and the Eucharist is more than just symbolism and ritual. In my late twenties, with so much coming up Catholic, I made a decision that looked and felt a lot like professional suicide—losing a job, losing family members, friendships, and all kinds of things—but discovering that really the fullness of my faith as an Evangelical Bible-believing Christian was not something that I had to reject but just take to the next level, that there was more good news than I thought maybe ten or twelve years earlier.

And I think of Saul that way too, because we call him a convert, but he didn't convert from one religion to another. He converted from one understanding of Judaism as a Pharisee to a much deeper and higher understanding. Because he had always waited for the Messiah. But only later did he find out that He had arrived, and that he was persecuting Him by persecuting His followers. And so, for me, I wasn't just non-Catholic, I was anti-Catholic, in a loving sort of way. I tried to target my Catholic friends and help them to see the error of their ways until I discovered the error of *my* ways, my anti-Catholic ways. And so in '86 at the Easter Vigil in Milwaukee, I was received into the Church, and it's just been an ongoing conversion since then, as it was for Paul.

Marcus: In case the audience doesn't know the deeper story, *Rome Sweet Home* came out in 1993, and you and Kimberly wrote that together.

Scott: We did. In three weeks, with a lot of prayer and tears and laughter and editing each other.

Marcus: There's something else that I want to mention before we go on to these other topics. I remember from your story, and this affected me a lot on my own journey, that one of the key places for you in your journey was the first time you went into Mass, and you saw the Bible come alive. I'm thinking that there's an awful lot of people, Catholics, that go into Mass, and they don't see it. To me, that emphasizes our need for catechesis and Scripture and knowing our Faith so that the Mass comes alive.

Scott: That's right. The Bible alone is not enough. But the Mass alone without any biblical literacy can often fall short. I think back to when I first converted as a teenager in high school. Fresh out of juvenile court, I needed the gospel. But I remember going to a Bible study that was tackling the book of Revelation. Bad idea, starting in the back of the Bible with the hardest book of all. But we spent months speculating about the antichrist, the Second Coming, and then I went to a second Bible study about a year later, and they were doing the same thing only from a different vantage point. I gave up after a little while and just went back to the Gospels and read the Bible all the way through a couple of times in high school. In college, I remember taking advanced Greek and being assigned in a tutorial the translation of the entire Apocalypse, all twenty-two chapters. When I was done, I still didn't know what John was talking about, but I was going on to seminary, it didn't matter.

But I remember when I went into Mass for the very first time. I was a doctoral student; I'd been studying the Fathers; I had been going deeper; I had been finding so much truth about the Eucharist, about Baptism, about the saints, and the seven sacraments. But I never once darkened the door of a Catholic church to attend Mass, and I didn't want to, but I was curious enough when I found out that it would be a midday Mass in a basement chapel. That sounded safe, so I went with a Bible and notebook, but I had no preparation for how scripturally saturated the Mass would be. I mean, from the opening rite, through the penitential rite, to the Liturgy of the Word—it was the Old and the New—it had been a year or two since I had heard that much Scripture. And then in the second half of the Mass, the Liturgy of the Eucharist was where the Scripture just took off. As soon as I heard, "Lamb of God Who takes away the sins of the world," I'm flipping to the back of the New Testament, looking at the book of Revelation, where Jesus is called Lamb twenty-eight times in twenty-two chapters, and I never knew why.

And as I'm looking at "Lamb of God," I'm seeing "Holy, Holy, Holy," and there's the Alleluia, the Amen, liturgical songs and prayers. Basically, the Mass finally made the Apocalypse understandable, and for me, the Apocalypse is what illuminated the mystery of what was taking place in the Mass. We were going to Heaven, whether we knew it or not. The angels and saints were surrounding us.

Marcus: This is the year of St. Paul, and in some ways, it was a good choice to call your institute St. Paul's Institute because it really connected everything. God's calling you to recognize the beauty of St. Paul in his writings but also his conversion. In what way have you come to see St. Paul's conversion itself as truly unique?

Scott: Well, it's been said that St. Paul was such a great apostle because Saul was such a great persecutor. God just simply redirected and harnessed that energy in a proper direction. Saul was the Pharisee who hunted Christians down to arrest them and put them to death until he met Jesus on the road to Damascus. But Jesus doesn't ask him, "Why are you persecuting My followers?" He says, "Saul, why are you persecuting Me?" (see Acts 9:4). And think about the mental gymnastics that this poor Pharisee had to go through, even while getting blinded suddenly. He's like: "Well, first of all, Who are You, Lord?" "I'm Jesus whom you're persecuting" (see Acts 9:5). Okay, and he's thinking:

"Well, I'm not persecuting You, I'm persecuting Your follow-ers, but You're the Lord, and You seem to take it pretty personally."

In the first century, there is only one Christian author who speaks of the Church as the "Body of Christ." And guess who it is? St. Paul. Because Saul the Pharisee discovered that the followers of Jesus aren't just embracing a theory or a group of opinions. They have been united to nothing less than the Lord of Lords. So, Saul discovered that, yes, he accepts the Word of God, he's doing his very best, but he's missing something very important. I can relate to that because as an anti-Catholic, I was simply following the Bible, or so I thought, until the Bible illuminated the mystery of Christ in the Eucharist, and at that point, I'm like: "Wait, all bets are off. I'm going to have to go back to the drawing board and rethink all of this."

And you know, Saul took three years shortly after becoming a Christian, getting baptized, to spend time in prayer and study in Arabia. I remember spending three years in intensive study in prayer, doing doctoral research while I was going through this process of entering the Church, and I can see the need, because suddenly you're rereading passages that you have read and taught, some-times dozens of times, only things are jumping off the page, and you wonder, "How could I have missed John 6, about the Eucharist? How could I miss Romans 6, about Baptism? Or Matthew 16, about Peter and the rock and the keys of the Kingdom?" These were the sorts of things that I discov-ered, and I can't help imagining that Paul, as a newly baptized Christian, went back and reread the Law and the Prophets and just probably wondered, "How could I have missed Jesus?"

Marcus: We often think of St. Paul as this great evangelist and missionary and writer but maybe don't appreciate the fact, just like you mentioned earlier, that it was committing suicide for his career. In Acts 6:7, there's an interesting statement which doesn't deal with Paul but the priests, where it says, "And the word of God increased; and the number of the disciples multiplied greatly in Jerusalem, and a great many of the priests were obedient to the faith."

Scott: It's so good that you bring that up because we read those kinds of verses over and over and never really get it. Here is the chief priest labeling Jesus a false Messiah, a blasphemer, using Roman authority to have Him executed. And then here are the priests who are under the chief priest, reaching a decision where they're saying, "We just murdered the Messiah. We didn't just miss Him; we had Him executed. And now we're going to join His cause." The chief priest is not going to look at that and say, "Well, we'll go our separate ways." It's not surprising that in Acts 6, the first priests are described as converting to the Way and getting baptized, and in Acts 7, we have our first martyr who was executed in Jerusalem, Stephen. At the end of that account, in Acts 7, you have Saul giving consent to Stephen's martyrdom, which doesn't mean he was just standing by nodding; it means that he was probably semi-officially sponsoring this sort of lynch mob.

Marcus: He was a top student. In fact, when you think about it, some of these other priests had gone that way, and he was probably belittling them.

Scott: Exactly. He would have been so provoked in his spirit to see priests defecting to that cause. "These men are fishermen from Galilee! We've got the experts in the Law here. How could you?" If you were the Lord God Almighty, and you were to single out one guy for conversion and give him that spectacular grace, who better than the greatest student of the greatest rabbi? Because if you're going to send the gospel out to the Gentiles with fishermen, you can expect the rabbis to say, "Well, what do you expect? They're fishermen from Galilee." But when our best rabbi's prized pupil goes out claiming that the Law and the Prophets point to Jesus and the Church as the fulfillment of these messianic prophecies and so on, then suddenly everybody's going to sit up and take notice and say, "We have got to take this thing seriously."

Marcus: I wonder what happened to the career of Gamaliel?

Scott: He gives wise counsel to the Sanhedrin not to persecute the Church, but it doesn't look like they were altogether convinced.

Marcus: There're so many issues that we could talk about with St. Paul, and for this year of St. Paul, we're just whetting the appetite. Talk a bit about the relationship between Paul and the Sermon on the Mount, and maybe explain why there's an issue there first of all.

Scott: Let me explain the issue first, because I think a lot of Catholics approach Paul differently than they approach Jesus and the Gospels. Jesus and the Gospels, for most cradle Catholics that I've known, is like a home game, and you win most of those. Whereas St. Paul is more like an away game, and you win a few, but you don't win most, especially if you're a hired fan from Pittsburgh or Steubenville like I am. The away games are really hard. Well, the fact is, as a Protestant, I felt similarly, only the opposite, because when I would read the Gospels, I'd be like: "Okay, there's a lot of emphasis on righteousness and works and obedience and giving alms and fasting and all of that," but no wonder, because that all was before Jesus' death and Resurrection, and so He was just reminding them of the Mosaic Law and the burden that it places upon the believer so that you end up kind of exchanging that Law for this gospel. And I thought, as you move from the Gospels to the epistles, you're moving from the end of the Law to the beginning of the gospel.

For me, Paul was the archetype. He was the source, he was the one you go to, to really understand the truth after Jesus' death and Resurrection. But to be honest, the "gospel according to St. Paul," which for years I interpreted as Evangelical Bible-believing Christian Calvinism—I had been trained to read Romans that way and Galatians that way—when I went deeper, when I got the Greek and I could read the original, when I studied the Hebrew and I could read the background that Paul was drawing from in the Old Testament, the Scriptures of ancient Israel, that's when suddenly I got beyond the superficial and I began to realize that Paul is thinking like a Catholic. In Romans 5, he deals with Original Sin. But in Romans 6, the way out is not just to accept Jesus Christ as your Savior and Lord, but to get baptized, because when you're baptized you die and rise with Christ. Not just symbolically, but somehow spiritually and actually.

And I thought, "If I were to write Romans, I would never have said that." He zagged when I would have zigged. I would have gone from Romans 5 into inviting Christ into your heart as Savior and Lord. That's language that Paul never once uses anywhere in his epistles, and he's writing half the

New Testament. You'd think that the Holy Spirit could have
led him to say: "The way you're saved is inviting Christ into
your heart to be your Savior and Lord, and once saved,
always saved"—none of which was found there in his writings. So, when I went back and rethought this, that's when I
began to realize there is a strange convergence between what
Christ is teaching in the Gospels and what Paul is teaching
in the epistles. For example, Matthew 5–7. Jesus teaches in
the Sermon on the Mount—His first public sermon—all
about the Fatherhood of God. Seventeen references to God
His Father in His first sermon. That's more references to
God as Father than in the entire Old Testament. Well, if you
read Paul's letters, they're just filled with references to God
the Father and Christ the Son.

For Saul the Pharisee to write that way would have been
unthinkable. Only after you encounter the eternal Son of
the eternal Father do you realize that all the language of
God as Father in the Old Testament wasn't metaphorical, it
wasn't figurative, it was real; but you only come to know it
with the coming of the Son. So, the Fatherhood of God, the
family of the true believers, that's one thing. Jesus also says
in the Sermon on the Mount that unless your righteousness
exceeds that of the scribes and the Pharisees, you won't
enter the Kingdom. Saul the Pharisee would have said,
"Ouch! You're stepping on my toe. What do you mean
unless your righteousness *exceeds* the scribes and the
Pharisees?"

But Jesus goes on to say, "You've heard that it was said to
men of old, 'Don't kill, don't commit adultery.'" That's the
civic code of Israel that establishes good citizens. Jesus says,
"But I say to you ..." And He's not talking about a civic law
that establishes good citizenship, He's talking about internal-

izing that law so you don't get angry, so you don't give in to lust. He's talking about becoming saints. That's the righteousness that goes beyond the scribes and the Pharisees. That's exactly what Saul had to kind of wake up to and realize: that when the Father sends the Son to give us the Holy Spirit, now, it isn't just a promise, it is a *fulfilled* promise that, through Baptism, makes us partakers of the divine nature. It draws us into a closer relationship with God than even Moses on top of Mount Sinai enjoyed. That's dramatic. But it also shows the profound convergence, the resonance, the deep agreement that you find between Jesus on the one hand in the Gospels and Paul in the epistles.

Marcus: It's a false dichotomy. Maybe a simple way to summarize how I used to think of it is that, before the Cross, it was about *my* righteousness, and after the Cross, it was about the righteousness of Christ. Before I was trying to be saved by my righteousness, but after the Cross, I point to His righteousness.

Scott: You've just paraphrased Philippians 3. In the Old Testament, the ancient Israelites properly treasured the Word of God, especially the Law of God, written with the finger of the Lord on these tablets of stone — I mean, what more could you want? Well, the *Word made flesh*, dwelling among us. He's assuming what is ours, human nature, to give us what is His: divine nature, divine sonship. So, Saul, now Paul, says in Philippians, "Whatever gain I had, I counted as loss for the sake of Christ" (Phil. 3:7). So, "it is no longer I who live," he says in Galatians, "but Christ who lives in me" (Gal. 2:20).

And to me, that is another breakthrough, because Christ didn't come in order to obey the Law, suffer, die, and rise in order to get us off the hook so we don't have to obey (although it's a great thing to do), or so we don't have to suffer (but we will if we don't have enough faith). No, Christ doesn't come as a *substitute*. In the Catholic tradition, following Paul, He comes as a *representative*. Christ comes and assumes what is ours, human nature, to give us what is His, divine nature. So He obeys—not in order to get us off the hook, to exempt us from obedience, but to empower us with His Spirit, to reproduce in us nothing less than His own divine Sonship, His own love, His own willingness to suffer, die, and rise. That notion of Christ the representative is much closer to Paul than Christ the substitute. We participate through the Spirit in Christ. And so, the Spirit comes to us, and especially in the Church, through the sacraments. As Paul taught, we end up receiving nothing less than Christ's own divine Sonship. That's just cool.

Paul, on the one hand, he's very practical, he's very personal, and yet suddenly is very profound and very passionate. Sometimes people who are passionate aren't very profound, and people who are profound are boring. But if the truth grips you, how can you not be passionate about the truth, and what is more passionate? What is worth getting more passionate about than this divine grace?

Marcus: I want to throw an idea and see what you think, and that is Paul's emphasis on the Law. I've found in the fifteen years I've been a Catholic that I spent most of those years dealing with converts. That wasn't necessarily my choice, but that was God's choice. And what I've found is that often converts, after they come to the Church, what they focus on and emphasize is what represents a counter-action to what they used to focus on.

So, you have James focusing on one thing, maybe because of where he came from, and Paul ... Is that why Paul focused on the Law, because he came from being such a high-level Pharisee?

Scott: I think you're right. I think the reason Paul focuses on how we are not under law but under grace is because he, more than any other contemporary of his, saw himself under law, and that was the source of his identity, that was the source of his righteousness, and that's how he understood grace. We didn't deserve God giving us the Law. Yet He spoke the Word; He wrote the Word; He's delivered His will to us. I mean, this is undeserved favor. That's grace in the Old Testament. But when you discover that the Word is now made flesh, that the Father sends the Son to give us the Spirit to adopt us and make us members of a divine family, then suddenly the graciousness of a law that we didn't deserve is exceeded infinitely by the graciousness of the Son, Who becomes the servant in order to make servants nothing less than divine sons.

In Romans 7, he speaks of the Law as holy, just, and good. And in Romans 8, where suddenly he just turns on the fire hydrant, you find more references to the Holy Spirit than anywhere else in the New Testament. I think it's seventeen or eighteen references to the Holy Spirit in Romans 8. But the Spirit comes to us why? "In order that the just requirement of the law might be fulfilled in us, who walk not according to the flesh [—bound just to the Law—] but according to the Spirit" (Rom. 8:4). So, the Holy Spirit comes to us to empower us to do what we could never do in the Old Testament on our own: keep the Law and fulfill our Father's will.

Marcus: When you interpret Paul's letters, how important is it to be looking at them through Catholic eyes—for example, understanding Ephesians as a document about Baptism—understanding Catholic things from this Catholic early Church background?

Scott: When you really begin to get the inner logic of Romans or Galatians or Ephesians, or 1 and 2 Corinthians, you realize that Paul's reasoning holds together according to a logic that is Catholic. And at times it's not just implicit. At times, he just comes right out and says things that I wonder: "How would I affirm that sort of thing as a Protestant?" For example, in 1 Corinthians 11, where he speaks of how you profane not a symbol of Christ's Body, you profane the actual Body of Christ when you receive the Eucharist unworthily, without discerning the Lord's Body. I know I had a clever response, but I would never have written those words the way Paul did.

Marcus: Sometimes I find myself, as a convert, on my *Deep in Scripture* radio program, emphasizing certain things in *contrast* to what I used to emphasize. But we Catholics need to read the Bible too! Ephesians 4 talks about how "the apostles and the teachers and the evangelists are for the equipping of the saints for the work of the ministry" (see Eph. 4:11–12). There we see the structure in a Church where it isn't just the leaders in the Church, it's not just their job, but it's ours too.

Scott: That's why it isn't like we emphasize a sacramental bond as *opposed* to a personal relationship with Jesus Christ. The sacramental bond that we celebrate in the Holy Eucharist should lead us to the deepest conceivable personal relationship with Jesus, the Lover of our souls, Who feeds us with His Body, Blood, Soul, and Divinity. It isn't like, "Well, you have the Bible; we have Tradition." We have Tradition so we can go into the Scriptures with greater freedom and greater confidence and find the truth in its fullness. Likewise, faith and works. We have faith in order to really trust God's Word and His Spirit to reproduce Christ's works in us.

Marcus: The Scripture that to me is one of the most powerful summaries is Ephesians 4:22–24: "Put off your old nature which belongs to your former manner of life and is corrupt through deceitful lusts, and be renewed in the spirit of your minds, and put on the new nature, created after the likeness of God in true righteousness and holiness." In a sense it's a summary of all that He wants to do to make us truly—dare I use this word—divine. Some in the audience may be shocked that we use that word, because they may not understand what we mean by it.

Scott: You can use it. Saints and Doctors of the Church do.

Marcus: The whole point is to be not gods but children of God.

Scott: And not just in name but in reality. As 2 Peter 1:4 says: "[We have] become partakers of the divine nature." Our adoption is not a legal fiction. God becomes human so that humans can partake of this divine nature. This sounds so speculative, almost philosophical, and yet for Paul, as you point out in Ephesians 4:21 and following, this is the most practical and the most demanding for our personal lives. But he wouldn't have gotten to those verses in Ephesians 4 unless he had laid the foundation in the first half of the chapter, where he says, "There's one Lord, one faith, one God and Father, one baptism, one Church, one Body" (see Eph. 4:4–6). And so, it's the unity of the Church. Which doesn't institutionalize our experience of Christ; it actually deepens how much of a personal relationship we as individuals can have with the Lord of Lords.

Marcus: I remember when I was a Protestant minister, I used to say that Ephesians 1–3 describes what happens after you accept Jesus as your Lord and Savior, and then chapters 4–6 are what you have to do now that you've accepted Jesus as Lord and Savior. When you understand historically, chapters 1–3 are what happens in Baptism. That is what Baptism does to you, and it's a reality.

Scott: That's right. He didn't say, "We *will be* seated with Christ in the heavenly places." In Ephesians 2, he says "*We are*" (see Eph. 2:6). We can't see it because we walk by faith, not by sight, but what the Holy Spirit does in uniting us to Christ through Baptism—if we could see what our guardian angels see, we would fall over. The glory of the grace of God that Paul discovered through Baptism, in the Eucharist, in the life of this Mystical Body of Christ, it exceeds all words. I mean, he did his level best to put into words the truth, but he says in Ephesians 3: "When you read this, you realize the revelation of the mystery that was given to me" and then he says, "I'm the least deserving of all" (see Eph. 3:3–4, 8). And I think we both can relate to that.

Marcus: Isn't that the truth? In many ways, I think Ephesians 4–6 is especially for us Catholics because there're some Catholics that think, "Well, I was baptized, I've arrived." Because while everything that's in Ephesians 1–3 is true, now we have to live it out. And every time we bless ourselves with the holy water, we're renewing our covenant bond.

Scott: John Paul II has made this comment, and Pope Benedict as well, that there are a lot of Catholics who are sacramentalized but not evangelized, just like there are a lot of non-Catholics that are evangelized but they haven't been led to discover the truth and the power, the beauty of the sacraments. It's not either/or. They're really mutually reinforcing. If we could only grasp the gift of God and the sacraments, we would say: "If you want an intimate relationship, this is the bond."

Marcus: Scott didn't come to the show to promote a book, but I really want to take the chance to mention one of his newer books, *Reasons to Believe: How to Understand, Explain, and Defend the Catholic Faith.* I made sure all my sons have read this book, because it's not just a defense of the Catholic Faith that starts from scratch. It really deals with the whole issue in a very winsome way, and the reason I wanted my sons, who are good, strong Catholics, to read it, is that my oldest son is studying at a secular university, so I wanted to make sure he's prepared.

In fact, the other book which I read of yours recently with Ben Wiker, *Answering the New Atheism,* is an awesome book too.

Scott: Well, that book grew out of this book, because you could only deal with so much, and so I try to show the classical arguments for the existence of God, miracles, prophecy, the Bible, and then the Catholic Church, the sacraments. But with the aggressive forms of the new atheism in Richard Dawkins' *The God Delusion* and other sources, you realize that the next generation is now faced with a kind of fundamentalist atheism that is shouting, and it's really shrill. It needs to be answered in a way that is patient and penetrating. I couldn't do it in this book, and so Dr. Ben Wiker—a good friend of mine—and I sat down to work on this.

Marcus: He's great. Again, I had my sons read that because our students are encountering these at secular campuses.

Scott: We had students who graduated from our school who went off, read *The God Delusion*, and lost their faith.

Marcus: Let's take our first email, from Wisconsin: "Thank you for your excellent programs; your show is the highlight of our week. I'd appreciate your explanation of why the Gospel of St. Peter was rejected from the canon of Scriptures. Since we believe him to be the first pope, I don't understand why his gospel was not included. Thank you both for your excellent ministries and your examples to many of us converts."

Scott: This is an example of the secular propaganda that's out there, in a lot of different sources—public television, *National Geographic*. What about the Gospel of Thomas? What about the Gospel of Judas? And what about the Gospel of Peter? Well, if it had been written by Peter, you can be sure the Church would have accepted it, but it wasn't. It's a forgery. That's why it was rejected. Likewise, the Gospel of Thomas was not written by the apostle

Thomas. It was a Gnostic Gospel, it was a forgery, and it was used to present errors, Gnostic beliefs, as truths to get Christians to accept these. And so the Church had to really use a great deal of spiritual discernment in recognizing authentic apostolic writings from those that really weren't.

You also had some of the books that were included in the New Testament, 2 Peter, for example, James, Hebrews—they were antilegomena. In some circles, people questioned whether those were authentic, and the Church said, "Yes, these are authentic, they will be included." And then you have things like the Gospels of Thecla, Paul, Peter, Thomas, Judas, and so on. And universally, the Church recognized that these were fraudulent gospels.

Marcus: Let's take our first call, from Illinois. Hello, what's your question for us?

Caller: I am a former Catholic, and I'm now an Evangelical, so I know you understand where I'm coming from. Could you please explain the Catholic teaching in light of the New Testament regarding Purgatory?

Scott: First of all, Jews have always prayed for their dead, before Christ and up to this present day. C.S. Lewis was a believer in Purgatory, though he wasn't a Catholic. He and others have pointed out that if you're praying for your dead, and if they're in Heaven, they don't need prayer; and if they're in Hell, prayer is not going to do any good. So, where are they? Well, in Hebrew, there's a term *Sheol* that is not the same as what we would call *Gehenna*. Jesus speaks of hellfire as Gehenna. Sheol is the place where the righteous and the unrighteous went, and that's why the Jews have always prayed for them. So even if you don't have 2 Maccabees in your Bible, if you read 2 Maccabees 12, and you discover that the prayers for the dead are being offered, then and by Jews today, you can see why. Because they really believe that there were people who could benefit. Well, why? What was *Sheol* in Hebrew becomes *Hades* in Greek. Again, it's not to be confused with Gehenna.

Hades is an intermediate state. When it's translated into Latin, it's called *purgatorio* because it's a place of purgation, a place of purging, cleansing. Hebrews 12:29 describes God as a consuming fire. Now, we often associate fire with Hell, but actually the imagery of fire is more commonly used in the descriptions of Heaven, because that's where the seraphim, the burning ones who are the closest angels to God—*seraphim* literally means in Hebrew "the burning ones"—they're burning with the pure love of God. We have to be filled with the Spirit to have that love purify us, and in this life we have our chance to really follow Christ. But you'll notice that Paul states in 1 Corinthians 3 that there are some people who build on a foundation of Christ with gold, silver, and precious stones, through works that really represent the Holy Spirit, reproducing Christ in us. Other people, Paul describes as building with wood, hay, and straw. That work, he says, will be burned up, but he goes on to say this, and it's so important: "If the work which any man has built on the foundation survives, he will receive a reward. If any man's work is burned up, he will suffer loss, though he himself will be saved, but only as through fire" (1 Cor. 3:14–15).

So, he will suffer, and he will suffer and lose, as he passes through the fire of the Spirit, Who will purify all of these false good works. Now, if time flies when you're having fun, time slows down when you're not. When you pass through the fire of judgment, which exposes the false, the inadequate, or the superficial good deeds that you've done, when you pass through the fire of God's love as judgment, that might take you five minutes, but it might feel like a lot longer. Paul is describing people who are going to be saved but only as they pass through fire, and they will suffer loss, but they will be saved on the Day of the Lord Jesus.

What struck me as a Protestant was, if I had a thousand epistles to write, I would never have penned those verses, I would never describe someone who's passing through fire, suffering, and yet they're going to be saved. Yet Paul, a good Jew and a good Catholic Christian, can write this sort of thing in a matter-of-fact way, just by way of reminder to kind of jog the Corinthian memory that we ought to be careful how we allow the Holy Spirit to build in our lives with gold, silver, and precious stones, and not the counterfeit works of those who are saved but are going to end up having to suffer a great deal as they pass through this fire.

Marcus: Where our Evangelical brothers and sisters often miss the point of that is their emphasis often on merely being saved or not. In fact, a good number look back to a time in the past when they were irretrievably saved or not, because "once saved, always saved," and so this whole concept doesn't fit their categories because they have that emphasis. It's also a different view of sin, what sin does.

Scott: Yes, indeed. Because sin is not just broken laws; sin is a broken life, a broken heart, a broken home, and so the Holy Spirit comes as the fire to restore that love. But we often say yes and don't mean it, or we say yes and then end up kind of turning our backs.

The Catholic doctrine was not something that I could understand, but I remember wrestling with this text, going back to the Jewish tradition of prayers for the dead, the Jewish notion of Sheol, the New Testament notion of Hades, which is not the same as Hell, or Gehenna. Then suddenly, I could see why the early Fathers would speak of a place like *purgatorio* as a place where the Spirit purges the leftover dross to purify the gold so that we can enter into the presence of God.

These people are going to be saved but only passing through fire and only after suffering loss. How could Paul write this, apart from believing in what the Catholic Church explains later on in terms of Purgatory?

Marcus: I can't remember which verses, I think it's in 1 John, but it talks about our desire to stand before Him without embarrassment (see 1 John 2:28). Well, that's why Purgatory. If we haven't lived perfectly in this life, then Purgatory is so that we can stand before Him without embarrassment, without hesitation, pure, cleansed, in the white clothing of the wedding feast.

Scott: Nothing unholy can enter the presence of God, and yet when we die, we sometimes have that lack of holiness left that the Holy Spirit has not yet completely uprooted.

Marcus: Let's take this next email from New Jersey: "Hi Marcus and Dr. Hahn. I returned home to the Church a year ago and am truly living my Faith for the first time. Unfortunately, I found myself face to face with a great deal of misunderstanding and at times anti-Catholic arguments and comments. Did you ever face this kind of reaction in your conversion? How did you best handle these disagreements, both personally and in apologetics?"

Scott: I would say back in '86, when I first decided to become a Catholic, I faced a tsunami—tidal waves in the plural—of opposition, and the first thing I would do was to remind my Evangelical Bible-believing friends that I, too, had been anti-Catholic and probably much more anti-Catholic than they were. And I would try to restate their arguments against the Catholic Church as well as I could, which was often better than they could because I used to hold them with such vehemence.

And then I would try, not to refute them in the sense of just beating them in an argument, but I would try to show how, as a Catholic, I'm not an ex-Evangelical; I feel *more* Evangelical than ever. I'm not an ex-Bible Christian; I feel like a whole new depth to Scripture has been shown to me. So, I would usually try to say, "Look, here's the common ground we share as Protestants and Catholics; it's much greater than our differences. Let's begin and end with the common ground, with the Bible, and let's move into those areas of disagreement, and I'll try to address your differences from my beliefs in terms of what we share in common." Because so often, I found in conversations that this not only fosters friendship and keeps ties from being broken, but it also shows them that it isn't something that requires the abandonment of all of the truths that you came to cherish as a Christian. It's not subtraction but addition. You're just discovering that they lead to even deeper truths about Jesus and the sacraments and that the Church is the family of God and so on.

Marcus: For those that are dealing with some of those issues, I would recommend *Reasons to Believe*, because that's exactly what you deal with in that book.

Let's take our next caller, from Massachusetts. Hello, what's your question?

Caller: Hi Marcus. My question is why did God change names in the Bible? Like when He changed Saul to Paul or Abram to Abraham or Sarai to Sarah? Thank you.

Scott: Good question. You have Abram getting his name changed in Genesis 17 to Abraham because there's a whole new calling and a whole new identity. You have Simon being renamed Peter because of a whole new identity and a whole new vocation. In the case of Paul, it actually isn't a divine name change, though. Saul was his Jewish name, and being a citizen of Tarsus automatically conferred Roman citizenship upon him. So, Saul is a Jewish name in Hebrew, but Paulus is the Roman name that reflects his Roman citizenship. But even though God didn't change his name from one to the other, God most certainly did use his Roman citizenship as well as his Roman name to launch this man to be the apostle to the Gentiles. Even while there isn't the same kind of name change, I think we can recognize in the book of Acts, as we move from Saul to Paul, we move from someone who's really clinging to the Old Covenant to someone who's discovered that the fulfillment of this has just opened God's family now to all the nations.

Marcus: We have an email from North Carolina: "Dear Marcus and Scott, how can I explain to Seventh-Day Adventists the reason why we Catholics worship on Sunday? They seem to accuse us of not following God's commandment of observing the Sabbath, by changing the Sabbath day from Saturday to Sunday. Please help me explain this, because I can't seem to find a biblical explanation for this. Thanks and God bless."

Scott: First, I want to recommend a book by a cardinal named Jean Daniélou. It was published fifty years ago by Notre Dame Press. It's called *The Bible and the Liturgy*, and what Daniélou does is to go back to the Old and New Testaments, and then the early Church Fathers, and show the significance of the seventh day and of the first day of the week, the Resurrection day, and how the Sabbath is transformed into Sunday as the Lord's Day.

And just to summarize what I learned from rereading him recently, as circumcision in the Old gave way to Baptism in the New, you have a bloody ritual leading to a cleansing ritual. Passover, an annual festival — slaughtering the lamb and eating that — is giving way to the Eucharist, which is the new Passover. In the Old Covenant, you worked and worked and waited until the Lord would send the eternal rest of salvation, and so, how appropriate it was for the first six days to be workdays and then the seventh day to be the day of rest because you were still waiting in anticipation for God to fulfill the promise of salvation or rest. But in the New Covenant, before we were working, before we're even born, God has achieved our salvation in Christ, who has, as Hebrews 4 puts it, achieved our eternal Sabbath rest. And how appropriate it is that all the Resurrection appearances occurred on Sunday. Not only was He raised on Sunday, but His appearances are all on Sunday.

So, in the early Church, as you move from circumcision to Baptism, from the Passover to the Eucharist, already in Acts 20 they gather on the Lord's Day, the first day of the week. In Revelation 1:10, "I was in the Spirit on the Lord's day." These casual references show us that there was a certain transition that was made pretty easily with the power of the Spirit guiding the apostles. So, the early Church didn't circumcise, but they sure baptized. They didn't sacrifice the lamb, but they celebrated the Lamb in the Eucharist. And likewise, it's not the seventh day at the end of our work, but the first day, because Christ has achieved our rest before we even pick up a hammer or shovel.

Marcus: All right, that's very good, Scott. Let's take one more call at least. This one comes from Wisconsin. Hello, what's your question for us?

Caller: Hello, my question is for Dr. Hahn. What I would like to ask is about your book, *Rome Sweet Home*. In a chapter written by Kimberly, she's talking to a former classmate of yours, and they were discussing John 6:63, where it says, "It is the spirit that gives life, the flesh is of no avail." And Kimberly explains that it's not cannibalism, as the people who walked away apparently took it to be, but rather that it's the resurrected glorified Body of Christ that we receive. I wondered if you're in agreement with that—is that the Catholic understanding?

And a second question—what translation of the Bible do you use?

Scott: The second question is easier. It's the RSVCE, the Revised Standard Version Catholic Edition.

The first question: I would say in John 6, when Jesus says, "Eat my flesh and drink my blood, and I will raise you up" (see John 6:54), and then He goes on to say that "the flesh is of no avail," "it is the spirit that gives life" (John 6:63), His point is not to negate what He previously said. When He says, "The flesh is of no avail," He doesn't say, "My flesh is of no avail." He's speaking about the flesh, *our* flesh. So, when He says, "My flesh is food indeed, and my blood is drink indeed. He who eats my flesh and drinks my blood abides in me, and I in him" (John 6:55–56), what He then says in verse 63 is what makes His Flesh so different from our flesh—our flesh which is so weak, His Flesh which is so strong—it's the Spirit. "The flesh is of no avail," "it is the spirit that gives life." But the Spirit uses the instrument of Christ's Flesh and Blood to give us this divine life so that He abides in us and we abide in Him precisely through this Flesh, which communicates nothing less than the Holy Spirit. I hope that helps.

Marcus: We've got a couple of minutes left, and I'll ask you a final question for our audience.

What difference does it make whether we're Catholic or not?

Scott: In this year of St. Paul, I think what we can celebrate as Catholic Christians is not only the ecumenical common ground that we share, which is substantial, and we tend to neglect that, but how the truths of Scripture in general, and especially the truths of St. Paul's epistles, lead us to recognize that when he says in Galatians 3:28, "There is neither Jew nor Greek, there is neither slave nor free, there is neither male nor female," what he's talking about is that there's no second-class citizenship any longer, because God is fathering a family that is worldwide, international. The early Fathers had a word for that. *Catholicus.* One, holy, catholic, and apostolic Church. It's the catholicity of the Church that is the newness of the New Covenant. Up until Christ, He was fathering a family that was national. Now, it's international, it's worldwide. And we as Catholics, in the year of St. Paul, can come to a much greater appreciation for this birthright that we have in Baptism, this incredible grace that we have by having God as our Father, Christ as our Brother, Mary as our Mother, the saints as older brothers and sisters, and Rome as a kind of place that reminds us of our international unity.

I hope that gets at it, but to me, that is what's really so awesome about being Catholic.

Marcus: It seems to me that one of the largest heresies of at least the twentieth century and on into this one is this idea that all that's necessary is "Jesus and me." And it would seem to me that, at least as Catholics, we emphasize that Christ intended there to be the Church as the channel through which we receive the grace of salvation.

Scott: Our culture is steeped in individualism, and so easily and so frequently we just kind of project that. I think this vision of God's Fatherhood and of the Church as this world-wide family not only counteracts it, but trumps it. It's like, "Why were we just settling for a personal relationship when we can enter into this glorious communion?"

Marcus: As we close, Scott, what's the place they can get in touch with you on the Internet?

Scott: Salvationhistory.com is our website for the St. Paul Center. That is where you can find all kinds of tools and resources for Catholic biblical study and theology.

Marcus: All right, Scott. It's always great to have you on *The Journey Home*, and if I haven't said this before, I am so very grateful to God that your witness and Kimberly's came into my life, because it's what started my journey home to the Catholic Church.

Scott: I'm so grateful for your friendship and also for the amazing grace that God is giving through you.

Marcus: Thank you for joining us on this special episode of *The Journey Home*. God bless.

The Real Population Crisis

Interview with Steven Mosher
(June 2005)

Marcus: Welcome to *The Journey Home*. I have the great privilege of introducing to you men and women who, because of their great love for Jesus Christ, were drawn home to the Catholic Church. Now, sometimes their journey home doesn't begin with a love for Jesus Christ. Sometimes they have no faith in God whatsoever. But God, through His love for them, starts opening their heart, because of the situations that they're in, to the truth of the gospel and the truth of the Church. In some ways, that's like our guest tonight.

Our guest is Steven Mosher. He is the president of the Population Research Institute.

First, it's great to have you back on *The Journey Home*. And as I mentioned to you just before the program, intellectually, I couldn't stand up to what you are dealing with. It's such an important issue, which, sadly, far too many people don't know enough about. We live our lives buying into ideas out there that are false, that not only shape our lives, but, as you're going to tell us, shaped an entire civilization in different ways around the world.

But first, give us a five- or six-minute summary of your journey, and then we'll get into some questions.

Steven: Well, my story begins back in China. I was the first American social scientist allowed to go to China back in 1979. It was in 1979, when the Bamboo Curtain had just lifted, and for the first time, we were allowed to go in and see what the Communists had wrought in thirty years of ruling that country. I was coming from a secular humanist background. I'd been at Stanford University, and everybody at Stanford, whether they're majoring in biology or mechanical engineering, gets a minor in secular humanism. These elite institutions are places where it's hard to preserve one's Christian faith if one goes there with Christian faith.

Marcus: That's probably across the board in institutions like that, at least in our country here.

Steven: I think so. They're the high temples of secular humanism. So, I went to China with the typical secular humanist view that China was terribly overpopulated and that the best thing the Chinese people could do would be to reduce their number, and also that abortion was okay—it was a woman's choice, a woman's right.

Marcus: What year was this?

Steven: This was 1979. China had just opened up to the West, and I got to China in the middle of the beginning of the one-child policy. Now, everybody's heard about the one-child policy. Every Chinese couple in the cities, even today, is limited to one child, *when* the government says they can conceive and bear that one child. In the countryside, some couples are allowed two, but the one-child policy is still in place twenty-six years after it began.[5] When I was in the village, at the beginning of the one-child policy, the authorities came into the village and rounded up all of the women who were pregnant, and they determined whether or not that was the first pregnancy, in which case they let them go, or whether it was a second or third or fourth or higher order pregnancy. Those women they told to get abortions. The ones who refused were locked up, arrested, taken away from their homes and families and subjected to grueling morning-to-night propaganda sessions until they gave in.

Well, I went with them during this process, and remember I was a supporter of a woman's "right to choose." These women were being denied any right to choose anything. They were simply being told to get abortions. And I went with them, I remember, to the abortuary when the procedure was being done. Now, a lot of these women were in the second trimester of pregnancy, the third trimester of pregnancy, we're talking about women who are past the point of quickening, who are carrying viable unborn children—seven, eight, even nine months pregnant—and I was there when those abortions were done. And Marcus, you cannot be in a room where a late-term abortion is done and not know what it means. What happens is the baby is killed, and the mother is wounded physically and spiritually, and at that moment, I became pro-life. Because at that moment, I knew for certain what an abortion was, and I couldn't countenance it. It was as if I was standing on the Temple of the Moon in the days

[5] This interview was given in June 2005. As of January 2016, the law in the People's Republic of China has changed to allow all couples two children.

of the Aztecs and watching human sacrifice, or in Carthage in the Roman days and watching them throw babies to the end of the Temple of Baal. This was the killing of a living human being, and it was wrong.

Marcus: Did you talk to Chinese doctors who basically said that they were allowed to kill the infant as long as just a foot was left in the womb?

Steven: That's right. I said, "Is it legal to kill babies up to the point of birth?" And they said, "Oh, yes, as long as the baby still is in the birth canal, as long as it has one foot in the womb, so to speak, it's legal to take the baby's life at that point."

It may have been legal in China, but it was certainly morally wrong.

Marcus: And some were using injections?

Steven: They were using injections into babies already born, into the soft spot, the fontanel, directly into the brain, killing babies after birth. Infanticide was also a part of the program. So, I saw this, and this was a great evil. Now, I'd never come face-to-face with great evil before. I mean, we live in a very comfortable, confident society. Materially, we're very blessed, although sometimes it seems like a curse, but here was evil in its purest form. And if you confront evil like that, you either have to conclude the universe is mad, there's no rhyme or reason to anything, or you have to conclude that there must be a countervailing good, there must be a God, there must be something to balance this evil. And I didn't want to live in an insane asylum, and so I began to seek God. And that was the first step in the journey, becoming pro-life and becoming agnostic, not knowing where to find God but at least becoming a seeker.

The second stage came about through the intervention of a wonderful Benedictine monk, Fr. Paul Marx. Fr. Marx is eighty-five years old this year. Almost twenty-five years ago, he called me, and he said, "I would like you to come and speak at one of my conferences." He said, "I can't afford to pay you, but you can come, and you'll make some friends, and you can bring your books and sell some books." Best offer I had. The secular humanists weren't listening. They liked the idea that China was engaging in forced abortion; they thought that China had an overpopulation problem and that this is precisely what it should be doing. Fr. Marx disagreed. First priest I'd ever talked to in my life. Very soft spoken. I went to meet him, went to his conference, and I found myself in the middle of a whole host of wonderful pro-life people. Now, you know pro-lifers. These are people who are not out for any personal gain. They engage in this work, at great personal sacrifice often. They may be mocked by their friends and colleagues. Society doesn't welcome their efforts. The unborn babies that are saved will never know who interceded for them, who was the instrument of their salvation. So, they do this work with no thought of personal recompense. Wonderful people—kind, loving—the very opposite of the professors at Stanford University, one might say.

And then there was Fr. Marx himself. He taught me the Catholic Faith. He gave me my very first catechism—the catechism by Fr. John Hardon, a wonderful catechism. He founded the Population Research Institute in 1989. He invited me in 1995 to come and run it. So, I'm indebted to him for my vocation. He taught my wife and me natural family planning, and so we're indebted to him for our large family. I'm grateful to Fr. Marx in many different ways.

Marcus: I mean, you never dreamed that by going to China that confrontation with evil would set you off in a different trajectory. At the time, you probably didn't interpret it as God, but as you look back, talk a bit about that call of God.

Steven: This was the hand of God, and I think I'm very blessed in a way, because I can see the hand of God orchestrating my life in this fashion. Doors were closed to me when I came back and began speaking out against forced abortion. I was shunned at Stanford. I was asked to leave. They refused to give me the Ph.D. that I had earned. But other doors opened, the door opened by Fr. Marx, for example, the opportunity to do pro-life work, the opportunity to meet and marry the saintly woman who's my wife and to have with her a large family, and that's the third part of my conversion. I mean, my wife. As St. Paul says, it's a case of the sanctified spouse converting the unsanctified one. I was the unsanctified one, she was the sanctified one, and I held on tightly to her skirts, and that's the only way I've gotten to where I am today. And then the children began to come along. We have eight children at home, all born by cesarean section at the cost of heroic suffering on the part of my wife, and each of these children has had a lesson to teach us.

I mean, the children that came into our life, and I think the children that come into most people's lives, are the instruments that God uses to teach us lessons, to teach us patience and charity, love, to make us ready for His presence in Heaven. They teach you all the corporal works of mercy. They teach you the spiritual works of mercy. I like to tell my kids that the only corporal work of mercy I haven't done for them yet is visiting the imprisoned, and who knows what the future holds. Our Lord told us that whatever we do for the least of these, our brothers and sisters, we do for Him. Well, for those of us who are married and have children, the "least of these" are the little children who come into our lives, naked and we clothe them, hungry and we feed them, thirsty and we give them drink.

Marcus: We already have a phone call and email ready. Before we go, quickly tell the audience, if they want to find out more about the work that you're doing, to read about it, be inspired by it, what should they do?

Steven: Well, the Population Research Institute is a worldwide pro-life, pro-family organization. We have projects in China, my first love. We've started orphanages there, we built churches there, we just started a safehouse in China for women fleeing forced abortion. They can go and find sanctuary there. We do work in Latin America and Africa. They can find us on the web at pop.org. Pop is not me. I'm a pop. But this pop is *population*. And there's a lot of information there for anybody who's interested in the question of whether or not our problem is too many people or too few babies.

Marcus: Talk about that myth quickly.

Steven: Well, we don't need to talk about the myth of over-population; it's been in the air that we breathe for the last thirty-five years. We've heard about the population bomb. The population bomb never went off; it never will. Birth rates are in free fall worldwide; many countries are dying, literally dying, filling more coffins than cradles each year. Other countries have below-replacement birth rates, which means that the population will over time decrease, and decrease very quickly. And you know, we think of Latin America, for example, as being a land of large families — that's not true anymore. It was thirty or forty years ago. Today, the average Latin couple has two children, and so Latin America's population is leveling off and will begin decreasing.

Africa has an above-replacement birth rate, but it has the scourge of AIDS. Fifty million people in Africa have AIDS, and they will all be dead in the next few years. It doesn't take long to run its course in Africa because of malaria, typhus, typhoid, and other problems.

Marcus: What about here in the United States?

Steven: Well, we are better off than any other developed country. Japan is averaging 1.3 children, Germany about 1.4, Italy 1.1. These are historically unprecedented birth rates, they're so low. We're averaging about two children, and it's come up in recent years.[6]

Marcus: What's the replacement rate?

Steven: Replacement rate fertility is about 2.1. You need the average couple to average 2.1 children to maintain a steady population.

---

[6] More current population research data reveals that the United States fertility rate is now well below replacement level, averaging 1.78 during the years 2020–2023. According to the Institute for Family Studies, almost half of the world's population lives in nations with below-replacement-level fertility rates. See "U.S. Fertility Rate 1950–2023," Macrotrends, https://www.macrotrends.net/countries/USA/united-states/fertility-rate.

All of the developed countries are below that, and many of the developing countries—countries that are still poor—are at or below replacement-rate fertility. Even in countries where the birth rate is still higher than that, it is falling, falling, falling because of the influence of Western culture. MTV is everywhere. Hollywood is everywhere. So, we're exporting, whether we like it or not, the culture of Manhattan and Hollywood, even to relatively innocent and untouched corners of the world, and we're destroying families and producing barrenness as a result.

Marcus: Okay, let's take our first call, from Connecticut. What's your question?

Caller: Yes, I wanted to ask your guest, Dr. Mosher, to what extent did the encyclical *Humanae Vitae* influence his thinking and his journey?

Steven: Well, this is a brilliant statement, *Humanae Vitae*, issued in 1968. It is prophetic in the sense that it predicted, as a result of the acceptance of contraception, all of the evils that would follow. It predicted mass sterilization; it predicted abortion, which we got a few years later in the United States. It predicted the decline in family life; it predicted the rise in divorce rates; it predicted the degradation of women that we see in pornography these days. So, obviously it was an inspired piece of work. My favorite story about *Humanae Vitae* comes from Bishop Bruskewitz of Lincoln, Nebraska, because he was a young priest in Rome at the time, the Rome of Pope Paul VI, and he recalled a Mass at which Pope Paul VI recounted all of the encyclicals he had issued over the course of his papacy and commented on each one. And then he got to *Humanae Vitae*, "On Human Life" in English. He paused, looked down, and then said very softly, "I did not betray the truth." And he repeated himself again, "I did not betray the truth." There was tremendous pressure on him, not only from outside the Church, but from within the Church, to give way on this key teaching, and of course, God would not have allowed it to happen, but one can say that if the Church had given way on this critical point, things would be much worse than they are today.

Marcus: If you reflect on the big picture, the cause and effect behind all of this, talk a bit about how underlying all of this is listening to the wrong voices, listening to the wrong authorities, and part of that being the need for an authority you can trust.

Steven: Well, there are obviously tremendous distractions in the world today, even for people of faith. Our material standard of living has never been higher. It's easy to take the nightly news broadcast as gospel. It's not. It's often just sensationalism. Many people around the world have stopped reading the Book. I mean, one of the reasons for low fertility, the dropping birth rate in once-Christian Europe, is because Mass attendance is so low. You've got 25 percent of the people in Spain attending Mass every Sunday, and much lower rates of Mass attendance in France, in Germany, and if you don't read the Book, if you don't read Scripture, you don't call to mind the fact that God has told us over and over again that children are blessings.

Marcus: This is a great example of how listening to the wrong authority has a big impact, the story of how the whole one-child policy happened in China.

Steven: People think it came about because, well, the Chinese Communist Party has always been tyrannical, and one night it decided to impose a one-child policy on the Chinese people. Well, that's not the whole story. The story actually begins in Rome, Italy, in 1974. There was an organization in Rome, a secular organization, in no way associated with the Catholic Church—probably Masonic in large part—which published a report which became known as the "Club of Rome Report." It was actually written by a couple of systems engineers at the Massachusetts Institute of Technology here in the United States, and it predicted—this report did—that if the population continued to increase, we would start running out of minerals in the '80s and '90s, we'd run out of zinc and chromium and copper and the rest, we'd run out of petroleum in 2010, and by about 2050, civilization as we knew it would collapse. That was the "Club of Rome Report."

Well, in 1978, four years later, a Chinese systems engineer by the name of Song Jian was visiting Europe. Now, China had been in the grip of the Cultural Revolution for years. The Red Guards had been rampaging in the streets. Intellectuals had suffered; people like engineer Song had suffered. They'd been under house arrest; they had been persecuted by the Red Guards. This was his first trip outside the country in twenty years. He was anxious to find out what had been happening in his field of systems engineering over the past two decades, and he stumbled upon the "Club of Rome Report," and he thought, "Aha! I found it. The latest in Western science and technology. I'm going to take this back to China, and I'm going to apply it to the Chinese situation."

And he did just that. He went back to China, translated it into Chinese, and applied it to the Chinese situation and did his own computer projection showing that if China didn't stop increasing its population, the Chinese civilization would collapse in about 2050. He took this to the Chinese top leadership. They sat in awe as they watched the first computer projections they had ever seen, and when he finished, they said, "What should we do, Mr. Song?" And he said, "Well, we have to embark upon a one-child policy." And that's exactly what they did.

Now, the way they did it, by arresting women and by forcing them to have abortions and by massive propaganda campaigns, I mean, this is typical communist behavior. The way they carried it out was according to their own past practices, but the idea came from the radical environmentalism of the West, and what Song didn't know was that two years after the report came out, and two years before he read it for the first time, the head of the "Club of Rome" actually admitted that it was a fraud, that the numbers had been exaggerated, that it had been a case of garbage in, garbage out—they put bad numbers into the computer and got these bad results—and he said, "We were just doing this to scare the world's parliaments into addressing the problem of population." It was a fraud from beginning to end, but the Chinese people died in earnest.

Marcus: That scenario points in such a bold way at our need to examine who we're listening to. Where did that information come from? And I know that when I was a Protestant that believed that the Bible alone was sufficient for all issues of moral theology—I even at one time was in a Ph.D. program where I thought I was going to be a medical ethicist based entirely on Scripture. But the problem is, you know as well as I do, that the Bible-only people have opinions all across the board, contradicting one another on issues like this very issue, some of which involve promoting abortion and promoting contraception. Your image of Pope Paul VI making that statement is an image of why we're Catholic: the authority we can trust that will not compromise what's true.

Steven: And this is what drew me into the Catholic Faith: the fact that there was a solid foundation. Because what you find in academia today is a total lack of understanding of the really big questions. "What is God?" They reject the very existence of God. "What is the state?" They imagine statist solutions to everything. "What is man?" They imagine he came about from some random collection of atoms. They don't understand the relationship between man and God and the state. They can't answer the big questions; they're busy playing in the shallows. They have no authority. They speak without authority. You know, I study Chinese history, and throughout Chinese history, you see the rise and fall of dynasty after dynasty, and even the best well-founded dynasties only lasted a couple of hundred years, three hundred years at the most. And yet here you have this institution, the Catholic Church, which has gone through century and century and century, now beginning its third millennium. This is not a human institution. A human institution would have decayed long, long ago. This is a divine institution, headed now by our 265th divinely selected pope. What a wonderful thing to have, an authority like that, a center or heart of our faith in God.

Marcus: Let's go to this call from Texas. Hello. What's your question for us today?

Caller: Hi, Marcus. God bless both of you. I have a comment for Dr. Mosher, and I wish he would explain it to the public: how the contraceptive frame of mind leads to abortion and how people don't even realize it. Thank you both.

Steven: A good question, thanks. Well, this is something I learned from Fr. Marx, as I learned so many things, because Father always said that contraception led to abortion, and I'll tell you why. First of all, you have contraceptive failures. These contraceptives that are all over the markets are not 100 percent fail safe. They fail at a rate of 3 percent, 5 percent, or even higher. Condoms fail at a rate of 10 or 15 percent a year. So, you have contraceptive failure, but if you've got a contraceptive mentality, if you've already rejected in your mind the possibility of having children, what are you going to do when the contraceptive fails? Well, the next "logical" step is to consider an abortion, ending that child's life that you wanted to prevent from coming into existence in the first place.

Also, contraception encourages fornication; it encourages sexual activity before and outside of marriage, and *that* leads to higher rates of abortion as well. I mean, we've got a very high percentage of women in this country who contracept. The abortion rate is not going down. The abortion rate is staying the same. Many of the abortions that are done are repeat abortions on women who were contracepting the first time, the second time, and are now back for their third abortion. Worldwide, we have raised the contraceptive prevalence rate. I say *we*, being the United States, because we fund this to the tune of billions of dollars a year. We have raised the use of contraceptives up to about 65 percent, and yet the number of abortions worldwide continues to increase. Contraception leads to abortion. It doesn't reduce the rate of abortion.

Marcus: And there's also the fact that some contraceptives are really abortifacients.

Steven: Absolutely. For every surgical abortion you have in the United States or around the world, and we're talking about over a million surgical abortions, you have also chemical abortions caused by the birth control pill, caused by Norplant, caused by Depo-Provera, and the IUD, which is still in use in many places in the world and doesn't prevent conception at all. All it does is prevent that tiny human being, that embryo, from implanting in the womb, so it's not a contraceptive; it is solely abortifacient. Someone wearing an IUD can conceive two or three or four children a year, and each one of those children will die when implantation fails.

Marcus: Not only are contraceptives not effective at preventing birth or abortion, they're also not effective at preventing disease either. Talk about Africa and the issues you deal so much with there.

Steven: We have been trying to help the African bishops deal with the scourge of AIDS, and the African Church has the only effective program against AIDS because it emphasizes marital fidelity, as the Church has always taught, and it emphasizes chastity before marriage and chastity within marriage, chastity properly understood. The Church has the answer to the scourge of AIDS. The answer given by the secular humanist is to promote sex education and condom use. This is spreading the disease; it's not preventing the disease. And when you talk about these chemical contraceptives like the birth control pill and Depo-Provera, you're actually giving women a progestin-based drug, a powerful steroid-based drug that thins the vaginal lining and thins the lining of the uterus, making it more liable—not less liable—to infection, so the disease may be spread in that way as well.

Marcus: Let's take our first email. This comes from Flushing, Michigan: "Is the right of women against forced abortion one of the rights listed as a basic human right by the United Nations or any international political organization? Or is the right of women only being defended by religious organizations?"

Steven: Well, let me tell you a little bit of personal history here because when I came back from China—and remember I was pro-life but still a secular humanist—I first thought to go to my secular humanist friends, my pro-choice friends, the members of the National Organization for Women, for example, because they talk all the livelong day about a woman's right to choose, and here clearly, the women in China were being denied the right to choose, so I thought they would be sympathetic to women in China. I remember speaking to the head of the National Organization for Women, and when I got all done recounting the evidence—I had pictorial evidence, I had audiotapes, I had manuscripts proving forced abortion for sterilization—she said, "Well, I'm personally opposed to forced abortion, but after all, China does have a population problem." And she wouldn't touch the issue after that.

Now, the U.N. charter on human rights does not mention the right to have children as a human right, I think because it was so basic a right that no one in 1948 imagined that it would ever be called into question. But the U.N. Population Fund, in its charter—this is an organization that was set up in 1968 to deal with the so-called population bomb—does say that couples have the right to determine the number and spacing of their children, so there is something there, at least in the U.N. Population Fund charter. But you find people who are working on the population-control front very unconcerned about what's happening in China. Their response is just like the response of the head of NOW: "Well, China does have a population problem."

Marcus: I think I ran across an article you had written about UNICEF.

Steven: Well, unfortunately, this anti-people mentality has penetrated all of the U.N. organizations, not just the U.N. Population Fund, which was created for this purpose. But also, the United Nations Children Fund, the United Nations Development Program, and the other programs. And UNICEF has gotten involved in promoting contraception; it's gotten involved in providing family planning and population control as part of the U.N. system.

Marcus: So, all the little kids out there with their little boxes collecting money think they're going to help the children.

Steven: You shouldn't be doing that. There are many, many good causes to give money to. Don't give it to UNICEF. Do not trick-or-treat for UNICEF.

Marcus: Let's take our next call, from New Hampshire. What's your question?

Caller: I have a question for Dr. Mosher concerning his education at Stanford. You've mentioned that you became a secularist by default by going to Stanford. In reference to the universities today in their pursuit of science, do you see a lack of gratitude in the sciences toward truth, and thereby toward nature? How do you see this as causing people to disrespect nature in themselves?

Steven: Let's not overgeneralize here because about half of all sciences do profess a belief in God. And it depends a lot on the discipline. I had the misfortune, even before going to Stanford, of being in the biological sciences of the University of Washington in Seattle. And in biology, of course, they take evolution to be an article of faith, and so they reject a priori the existence of God. Then I went into anthropology at Stanford, which was just as bad because they are situational ethicists and moral relativists, and they believe that whatever any tiny human group decides to do should be morally acceptable, and if you don't accept that, then you're being ethnocentric. So, I probably saw academia at its worst. A lot of the physical scientists, a lot of the physicists, for example, and the chemists, the ones who actually work to discover natural laws in the way that processes work, do become convinced of the existence of a Creator by the simple fact that natural laws do exist. Who put those laws in place, and why is it that all of those laws work in favor of the existence of life, and particularly, human life? There are too many things going on at the same time for it all to be coincidence, and I think many scientists recognize this.

Marcus: It's almost to the point where some sciences are more pure sciences, like you mentioned, and some that — I even think in anthropology, some of the biology curriculum — almost become pseudo-sciences, especially in the psychology/psychiatry area, where they're theory based on theory based on theory based on theory. It's almost a form of Gnosticism where they start with one assumption, and slowly they've forgotten where they began. But they just assume it all without question, and that's not science, that's a form of religion in itself.

Let's take this email from Alexandria: "Hi Marcus and Dr. Mosher. How do we respond to our non-Catholic friends who ask how the Roman Catholic Church can justify banning contraception in overpopulated, underfed countries?"

Steven: Well, that takes us to the heart of the matter. That's a very good question. What is overpopulation? Well, the answer is we don't know. Demographers have never been able to define overpopulation. When people start talking about overpopulation, they usually conjure up images of crowded cities or slums. Sure, there are places in the world that are very densely populated, but there's no logical definition of overpopulation. How many people can the planet hold? How many people can the United States hold? How many people can the State of Texas hold? There's no way of knowing for a fact what the carrying capacity of the United States or Texas or the world is before you define what level of industry you've got, what level of technology you're able to use, and then you can come up with a number. How you're producing food, whether you're mechanized or you're out there with a hoe in the fields. I mean, hunter-gatherers can only survive at about the rate of two people per square mile. We have fifty or sixty thousand people per square mile in New York City. How do they all survive? They actually don't just survive, they do very well, because in the city, they have access to better medical care, better job opportunities, better educational benefits. People live in cities for a reason. They live in highly congested places because those places give them advantages that they wouldn't have on a desert island, for example. So, we have to be careful about assuming that any place is overpopulated.

Now, famine is still a problem in the world, but not because of a worldwide shortage of food. We have a worldwide *surplus* of food. Ask any farmer. Food prices keep going down further and further, and each time they drop, it makes life a little more difficult for farmers. We do have a problem of distribution in some parts of the world, but a brilliant Indian economist by the name of Amartya Sen got the Nobel Prize in economics in 1998 for showing that famine was ultimately a political problem, that the only famines that had occurred in the twentieth century were famines that had been brought on by government intervention into the economy, as happened in China in 1960.

Chairman Mao took the workers out of the fields, left the wheat crops and the rice crops to rot in the fields in many cases, and set them to work building dams and steel mills, and starvation ensued. And forty-two million people died. They didn't die because there was a shortage of food, initially at least. They died because of bad judgment and bad decisions on the basis of Chairman Mao, who, when the starvation began, refused to admit to the world that there was famine and refused to ask for help. Instead of swallowing his own pride, he let Chinese peasants die by the millions. That's what I mean by political famines. We see political famines, even today. They're not caused by shortage of food. They're caused by bad government.

Marcus: I was thinking about how people say we have a population explosion here in our United States, but all you have to do is take an airplane ride from New York, fly across the country, and just look, all the way to California, and there is plenty of land out there. If you went back 150 years, when towns were continuing to spring up across the United States—when they were republishing state maps probably every week because of new towns—that little town could be self-sufficient because of the mom-and-pop grocery store and the livery stable and all of that. And then you go start a new town, and everyone could work on that because it was locally centered. But with technology, we've destroyed that possibility in the United States. And so, that's why we're all conglomerating like ladybugs. In our part of the world, the ladybugs creep into the house and cram into a corner. I mean, that's what we've become like. But we can't spread out because we've become so attached to this way of life that we don't want to give up.

Steven: I was talking to a fellow from New York City a couple of years ago, and he was complaining about the fact that there were too many people in the world, and yet he voluntarily chose to live in the largest city in the United States. Why? Because there were advantages to doing so. The center of the country is emptying out. I mean, the Dakotas are losing population; Nebraska and Kansas are close behind. Cities, towns are shrinking and dying in that part of the country. When the local school goes, of course, the town generally ends. They're running football teams with not eleven players now but only six players because they don't have enough high school boys to field an eleven-man team.

Marcus: The trajectory of this is not promising.

Steven: Over the long term, it means extinction. For example, Italy. If you're averaging only 1.1 children, a little over one child for each couple—what does that mean for the Italian population? Well, it means that it's going to be cut in half, each generation. I mean, I like the Italians; I'm going to miss them, but if they don't start having children, they're gone.

Marcus: Well, isn't that what's underlying the whole Social Security issue that we're looking at here in the United States?

Steven: I see the debate in Congress, and I think we're just temporizing; we're talking about intermediate solutions. Sure, we could push back the age of retirement, we could raise the taxes a little bit, we could lower the benefits, we could bring more women into the workforce, we could have the elderly work longer. But all of those just mask the underlying problem, which is that we're having too few children, we're raising too few children up to be future taxpayers, future contributors to the Social Security system. And we at the Population Research Institute have actually done a study showing that if we could get the birth rate in the United States back up to where it was before *Roe v. Wade*, before the legalization of abortion, at about three children per couple, then the Social Security system, as currently set up, would not be compromised forever, it would be solvent forever. So, the basic problem is to raise the birth rate, encourage young couples to have children, and the problem goes away.

Marcus: Let's go to this call from New York. Hello. What's your question?

Caller: I was wondering how much effect the United Nations program and commissions around the world have on the increased abortion rate in third-world countries?

Steven: The U.N. Population Fund has a tremendous influence in the third world. The U.N. Population Fund brags about being the largest supplier of contraceptives in the world, and it is. Closely behind the U.N. Population Fund is our own International Agency for Development. But I have some good news on that front. For the last four years, the United States has not been funding the U.N. Population Fund because in 2001, an organization called Population Research Institute sent investigators into China to look and see whether or not the UNFPA was involved in forced abortion in China. We came back with the evidence showing that they were, and the Bush Administration cut funding that year and has cut funding every year since.[7] So, even though

---

[7] Unfortunately, this is no longer the case under the current U.S. administration. According to information published on the UNFPA official site, "UNFPA welcomed the return of the United States in 2021 as a key donor and champion of women's and girls' health and rights. The United States generously contributed $50.5 million in 2022 to UNFPA's core resources....

the U.N. Population Fund is out there promoting steriliza-tion, contraception, and abortion, we are not paying for it.

Marcus: Okay, let's take this email from Tampa, Florida: "I have heard that in the next few years, China will experience serious problems with care for the elderly since, traditionally, senior citizens have been cared for by their children. Soon, however, there will be not enough young and middle-aged adults to care for them. Also, aren't there a disproportionate number of males to females? Will they have to look outside of China to find marriageable females? Thank you."

Steven: Well, this is a huge problem for China. I mean, we look at the world today, and we have two different sets of problems. In the developed world, we have countries that grew rich before they grew old, and they're having difficulties with their pension programs. But you also have countries like China that have grown old, are growing old before they will grow rich, and they have no pension programs in place for about 80 percent of the population. What are they going to do when these massive numbers of people now enter old age with only one child to support them? It's a completely untenable situation. I'm very afraid that, in years to come, China will embark on another population-control program, kind of the polar opposite of what I saw. I saw young pregnant women being arrested and taken in for abortion, their babies targeted. I'm afraid the targets in the future in China will be the elderly.

The United States has contributed $10 million to the UNFPA Supplies Partnership, with a focus on providing contraceptives and life-saving maternal health medicines in refugee settings."
"United States of America," United Nations Population Fund, https://www.unfpa.org/donor/united-states-america.

Marcus: They haven't opened euthanasia out there?

Steven: Well, they have quietly begun a kind of stealth euthanasia program. You can't be admitted to a hospital in China today if you're elderly; they admit only people of working age. If you're elderly, they generally don't give you a bed; they tell you to go home. The other thing that's happened is there is now a euthanasia society that has been set up in China. Well, China is under the control of the Chinese Communist Party. These things don't just spring up out of the popular will. So this is the opening wedge, I think, of a campaign to legalize euthanasia, and when it happens, it'll happen in a massive way.

Marcus: You mentioned how the whole population issue started in China with one man coming out and reading something. Let's hope he doesn't come out and read *Soylent Green*. Hopefully, movies like that don't get taken back into a culture that has an "overabundance" of elderly people.

Steven: And a shortage of women. There are one hundred million[8] more men than women in China today, and about twenty-five million of those men are young men who are growing up and will not be able to get married, not be able to find brides because their brides have been killed.

---

[8] According to the Chinese National Bureau of Statistics, as of 2021, the disparity has dropped to about thirty million more men than women in China, with 17.52 million more men of marriageable age (twenty to forty years old) than women of marriageable age. "China Has 17 Million Men Looking for a Bride: National Bureau of Statistics," *Global Times*, May 17, 2021, https://www.globaltimes.cn/page/202105/1223654.shtml.

Marcus: What chance do you see of this eventually escalating into a military issue worldwide?

Steven: Well, I think China is a problem. First of all, because its economy is growing by leaps and bounds — we're helping in that regard. Secondly, because it remains a one-party dictatorship, so you have a partially free-market economy combined with a Leninist one-party dictatorship. What is that? It's not classical communism. It's national socialism. This is Nazism redux, happening again in China. That's the political system and the economic system that they've got today. Now, are they going to move in the direction of respecting human rights and democracy? I hope so, because if they don't, in about ten years, we will have another superpower confrontation. Already, China has looked at our national military academies as near-peer competitors.

Marcus: And sadly, more and more of our own money is being funneled into China as we buy more and more Chinese goods.

Steven: And on the one hand, you say, "Well, you're helping ordinary Chinese who work in factories to make these things to improve their lives." On the other hand, this is hard currency, it goes into the coffers of the central government, and it frees up resources for them to buy and borrow and steal weapon systems from overseas. So, it's a real concern. We have to pray for the conversion of China. The ultimate solution to this is the ongoing conversion of China, along with India, one of the last great unconverted countries in the world. We need to reach the Chinese people with the gospel.

Marcus: All right, let's go to this call from Louisiana. Hello. What's your question?

Caller: What is the Population Research Institute doing currently to engage in a public discourse on this issue? I'm in graduate school right now, and there's an inherent bias against the position you put forward. What specific activities are the Population Research Institute engaging in to create an informed public policy approach to this issue?

Marcus: Thank you. In fact, you point out a real problem out there, these underlying assumptions that are everywhere in our culture.

Steven: From the late 1960s, early '70s, we have been fed this in our social science textbooks and biology textbooks. It has been a government-funded campaign to convince us there are too many people in the world, and so for most people, it's just common sense to say there's an overpopulation problem. And when you say to them, "No, our long-term problem is not too many people, it's too few people," when you say to them, "The current numbers show that the population is going to peak in about thirty to thirty-five years at nine billion and then begin to decrease and decrease at an ever-increasing rate," and when you say that before that happens, the populations will age and pension funds will go belly up, it takes a while for them to absorb that. But those are the facts, and facts are hard things. We're doing all we can. I mean, one of the things we're doing is we're doing a series on EWTN on the global fight for life, taking people to Mexico, and dying Spain, for example—one of the shows is on dying Spain. Spaniards are averaging 1.1 children, just like the Italians. And we ask why that is and what can be done to reverse that trend.

Marcus: You know what, I hate to say it, but our politicians on both sides of the tables are so influenced by votes and contributors and lobbyists. Do you see any great champions out there that have recognized this as a myth and are willing to take a stand on the significance of this issue in our government?

Steven: Well, you know, when you talk about the U.S. Congress, you're talking about a herd mentality. Most of the people sit on the fence, and there are some who declare themselves to be pro-life back in their home states and back in their districts, but there are only about a dozen who will really lay down in the road and die for the babies, who really, in a sense, sacrifice political capital to save human lives, to rescue unborn children. And when you're talking about the population question overseas, the number is even fewer, but they are coming around.

We had an up or down vote a few years ago on population-control funding for the first time in thirty years. We argued that we should take one hundred million dollars of money, and instead of spending it on sterilization equipment and handheld suction abortion machines and abortifacient contraceptives, we should spend it on primary healthcare. What a radical idea. Let's save babies by giving them immunizations instead of preventing them from coming into existence. And it was a fairly close vote. I think we gave the other side a scare. And so, I'm confident in years to come that we can move the ball forward.

Marcus: How do you eat elephant? One bite at a time. It's a long, long process.

All right, let's take our next email: "I enjoy your show very much, and I am against contraception, but what about Africa with AIDS? Isn't it right to use contraceptives in this instance, since sixty, fifty million people will be dying from AIDS and many children will be left orphans because of it? Thank you, and God bless."

Thank you for your fine questioning. I know that expresses a concern for a lot of people.

Steven: It certainly expresses a concern of mine. I am continually distraught over the fact that there are fifty million people in Africa with AIDS, and we have to understand that AIDS runs its course very quickly in a population which is undernourished, where many women are anemic, where typhus and typhoid and malaria and yellow fever are endemic, where you don't have access to clean food, clean drinking water. It can kill you in two or three or four years, leaving the population bereft of people in their twenties and thirties. That takes the very heart out of the population. What do you have after an AIDS epidemic sweeps through a country? You have children, and you have grandparents. How do you develop an economy like that? But what do you do about this? How do you stop the disease? There's only one country that has been successful in not only stopping but reversing the AIDS epidemic, and that is Uganda. And what Uganda did was emphasize abstinence before marriage and fidelity within marriage, being faithful. In fact, you can see billboards today in the country of Uganda that say: "Zero grazing outside of your own field." That's Ugandan for "Be faithful to your wife." And they've dropped the AIDS infection rate from 13 percent down to 5 percent because AIDS doesn't rain on you, you get it from a certain kind of activity, or you get it from bad medical practice. You can only get it from either sexual activity or bad medical practice, and if you're faithful in a lifelong monogamous relationship, as the Church teaches, with one man or one woman, you're safe.

Marcus: Let's see if we can grab one last caller from Alabama. Hello, what's your question?

Caller: I was just wondering, with so many people who want to adopt children, could your guest sort of get us started on the right track for anyone that would want to adopt some of these unwanted children that are in China?

Steven: I think adopting little girls from China—because they're all little girls, they're not little boys, they're all little girls in the orphanages today in China—is a wonderful thing. I think that every baby adopted from China is a life saved, and I mean that. Because although conditions in the orphanages now are better than they were ten years ago, they are still very dangerous places for little baby girls. There are frequent epidemics. The babies die in large numbers. So, every baby adopted is a life saved, certainly a life saved from institutionalization, and it is possible to adopt baby girls from China. Not for me—I'm a spy in the eyes of the Chinese government. They won't let me in the country, otherwise I'd go there and come back with a baby under each arm. But any American can go to an adoption agency, one of the agencies that are active in China, and apply for adoption. And if our questioner would like, they can visit our website, and I'll send a list of agencies.

Marcus: Really quickly, let's take this last one because I'd like us to end on this because it is a very important email: "Perhaps you could say a few words on the state of the Catholic Church in China and the martyrdom going on there?"

Steven: Well, the martyrdom is a real thing, and there have been recent—just in the last couple of days—arrests of underground priests. The state of the Catholic Church, however, is very good. The number of converts is growing. There is a long history of the Catholic Faith in China. There are villages that have been Catholic for centuries. Those villages survive, the Faith is strong there today. The blood of the martyrs is the seed of the Church. The Church is growing in China. We don't know how many Catholics there are in China, but I would tell you this, that the Ministry of Education of the People's Republic of China admitted to a friend of mine a few years ago that there were eighty million Christians in China.

Marcus: I know that even some of those bishops that are appointed by the government ended up being faithful Catholics.

Steven: Right. Most of them.

Marcus: That's such a great miracle. Steven, thank you very much for joining us on *The Journey Home*. Thank you for your witness and for your work with the Population Research Institute.

The Conversion of Dietrich von Hildebrand

Interview with Alice von Hildebrand

(October 2000)

Marcus: Good evening and welcome to *The Journey Home*. My guest tonight is Dr. Alice von Hildebrand. Our focus tonight is on the conversion of her husband Dietrich, and many of you know him as a great philosopher. In fact, Dr. von Hildebrand released a book called *The Soul of a Lion*, about the conversion of Dietrich von Hildebrand. It's his biography. He is considered one of the great Catholic philosophers of the twentieth century. In fact, many consider him a Doctor of the Church already. If we had lots and lots of time, we could talk about his writings, his many books, and especially his particular angle on Catholic philosophy. But we're here to talk about his conversion. Many of you may not know that he was a convert to the Church.

Our theme for tonight became very obvious as Dr. von Hildebrand described her understanding of his conversion. The theme is the reality of the vertical dimension of life, the impact of the supernatural in our otherwise horizontal focus in life. We live in a culture that is primarily obsessed with the horizontal and blind to the vertical. For Dietrich von

Hildebrand, it was this awakening to the reality of the vertical dimension of God that changed his life, and, through his writings, changed so many others.

Dr. von Hildebrand, welcome. As I've mentioned, we've talked about having you on the program for a long time, although you're not a convert ...

Alice: I'm a cradle Catholic, but now that you've been a Catholic for a few years, you know how badly cradle Catholics need to be converted.

Marcus: Really every one of us needs to be a convert. Every single person needs to have a conversion, an awareness, an awakening, a hunger and a thirst to grow in holiness and follow Christ, a daily conversion, taking up our cross. And so, the journey home actually is not just about finding the fullness of the Catholic Faith, but it's about following Christ faithfully in every aspect of our life.

So, let's begin as usual. We're going to focus on your husband. Let's begin by setting the background for his spiritual life.

Alice: Well, he came from an extraordinary background. When I met him, I was a late-teenager. He was a refugee, living in total poverty. He had holes in his shoes; he had ill-fitting clothes. And one of the things that he said to me made an impression upon me: "I had a marvelous youth." The contrast was striking. He kept saying, "I had a marvelous youth." I found out that he was the son of a very successful sculptor who had an enormous fame in Germany and was even knighted by the king of Bavaria. He was born and raised in Florence, which is to my mind the most beautiful city that you can imagine. His father then built a house in Munich, a magnificent house. And he said to me many times, quoting *Lohengrin*, the opera of Wagner: "I don't come from darkness and sorrow, I come from splendor and delight." He was the last child of a family of six children, preceded by five sisters; he was the pet of his mother. He lived in beauty; there was joy. One of the very famous persons of the period said, "The house of von Hildebrand is a house of happiness; there is joy, there is light, there is love, there is friendship." And there was absolutely no trace of religion.

Both his father and mother were raised Protestant, but they did not practice. They never went to church; it never was mentioned. They never prayed, as far as we know, but surprisingly enough, their little boy had the extraordinary grace at the age of five of being convinced of the divinity of Christ. He was sort of religiously inclined, but he had no religious formation. And he said to me, speaking about his conversion, that he was very much like someone raised in a beautiful apartment, beautiful paintings, music in the background, and so on and so on, but that there was no sunlight. And then, one very fine day, something extraordinary happened to him, which was going to change his life radically. As a young man of seventeen, he went to the University of Munich, and soon afterward he met a fallen-away Catholic, Max Scheler.

Marcus: So, we've got Dietrich, seventeen or eighteen years old, from this very privileged background. Often when you hear people talk about their conversion — we might call it the caricatured conversion story — we're told how negative their life was before Christ, and then it's a great conversion to joy. But here's an example of a person who had what we might call a horizontal life of great beauty and great joy, great privilege, wealth, everything going for him. He was happy. So, if the theme we're looking at tonight is the interjection of the supernatural, the vertical element … at that age of seventeen or eighteen, given his background, did he have any concept of the vertical?

Alice: He was very reverent. He was open to a religious experience, so to speak. He was profoundly moved at the age of fourteen when he heard the *Passion according to Saint Matthew* of Bach. But you cannot say that he was devoured by a nostalgia of longing for something else, because he was happy, he was fulfilled, he was successful. He was enjoying life immensely. And then he went to the university and met this man, Max Scheler, who was a fallen-away Catholic but his teaching was still Catholic. I mean, there was a split personality because his life was unfortunately very bad, but his teaching was Catholic. And one fine day they became friends. And he said to my husband, out of the blue, "The Roman Catholic Church has the truth." And my husband was amazed. The Roman Catholic Church? He had lived in Italy most of his life, he had gone to many Catholic churches because they were beautiful, but he had never met a Catholic in his life who explained the Faith. And he said, "The Catholic Church? What do you mean?" Now, this is going to be key to my husband's conversion.

Scheler said, "Yes, the Catholic Church produces saints." Now, this boy, raised in Italy, he said, "Saint? What is a saint?" And Scheler had this genius for describing phenomena, and he sketched the essence of sanctity, of holiness, a total transformation of man's nature by and through Christ, by sketching the personality of St. Francis of Assisi. And I'm just going to mention two brief things of St. Francis, which, to my husband's mind, were absolute revolution.

What is perfect joy? Well, you're Franciscan and you go to a Franciscan convent late at night and you're drenched and you're hungry and the porter refuses to open and says, "You are knaves, you're fools, and I don't trust you. I'm not going to open." And you're freezing and hungry and you bang and you bang and you say, "Please, open to us." And the porter, who doesn't seem to be very holy, comes out with a stick and beats you and throws you in the snow. And Francis says, "This is perfect joy." Of course, from a purely secular point of view, it's madness. You're hungry and you're cold and you're beaten. And why is it perfect joy? Because Christ has chosen suffering in order to save us, and therefore suffering has an immense value and meaning, and suffering brings us closer to God.

Or take another example that my husband loved, when Francis had become enormously successful because of his holiness. And one day, one of his brothers said to him, "But Francis, why does everybody run after you? You're not particularly handsome. You are not a learned man; you are not outstanding in any way. Why do people run after you?" And St. Francis exulted in joy and said, "Because God could not find anyone more miserable, more wicked, more miserable from every point of view than Francis. This is what he showed me." Now, for my husband, that was an absolute revolution. He had a very keen ethical sense and suddenly a world opened to him, the world of supernatural morality, humility.

All of us, and I say all of us, are influenced by the New Age. And what is the New Age telling us? "You are okay, and I'm okay, and it's extremely important to love oneself and to like oneself and to feel good about oneself," and so on. Francis discovered that without Christ he was a spiritual beggar, that he needed to be redeemed, that he was nothing, and he rejoiced in being nothing because he knew he was infinitely loved. "Suddenly," my husband said to me, "I was coming to the sunlight." All the beauty that he had seen, all that *was* beautiful—and all of a sudden, the world of God opened up for him. And, of course, the two virtues which are the Christian virtues par excellence are humility and charity. And humility is to rejoice in my nothingness because I'm so infinitely loved by God Who is all powerful and can absolutely renovate and change me.

That was for him an absolute revelation, and he was on his way to conversion. But it took six years for him to enter the Church. He was taken up by his studies; he was the privileged student of Husserl—Husserl considered him one of his most talented students—he was engaged, he got married, he had a child.

And then all of a sudden, another thing happened that was going to be decisive. His second sister was married to an American who was living in Rome and had become an Italian citizen. He hadn't seen her for years. They had very little contact because he was at the university and she was in Italy. And suddenly he finds out she has become a Roman Catholic. Now, she was a very proud lady, handsome, talented, a remarkable painter. And of all his sisters, she was the one who was the least religiously inclined. She had said to my husband when he was a little child, "You know, Christ is quite a nice person, but for goodness' sake, don't compare him to Michelangelo or to Beethoven. This is ridiculous. These are *geniuses*, and he's just a good man." And she found Christ! She invited him and his wife to go to Rome to be there when she received her First Communion in the catacombs.

So the first time in his life he went to Rome, and this proud lady was kneeling down, begging God forgiveness for her sins, and he was just overwhelmed. And on the way back, she said, "You know, grace is knocking at your door and, if you don't answer immediately, it might not come back. *Promise* that when you go back to Munich, you're going to take instructions." And he went to Munich and started to take instructions. He knew nothing about Catholicism, and he drank it in like a sponge, all the dogmas, and he had no difficulty, absolutely none. There was only one obstacle, and that was artificial birth control. The priest who prepared him said that the Church prohibits artificial birth control. And my husband—he had a very strong ethical sense—he said, "*Why?*" He was absolutely amazed. "I mean, you're not killing, you're just preventing an egg from being fertilized." And the priest, he was a real priest, and he said, "Either you accept the totality of the teaching of the Church, or I don't accept you in the Church." Without a moment's hesitation, he said, "*Credo ut intelligam,* I believe in order to understand."

Now, it is interesting, because he was pretty self-assured—he knew that he was extraordinarily talented—and yet he never had any difficulty accepting the teaching of the Church. He said to me, "You know, that was for me the great revolution, the discovery of the supernatural. And the next moment, I discovered that there was an authority *above* me." He said, "Up to that time, I was the authority. When I saw something to be true, that was it. And all of a sudden, there is an authority that is not a human authority; it comes from God." And so he saw God, Christ, His Son, His divine Son, giving this authority to the Church. So when the Church teaches, it is not a human teaching; it a divine teaching, and all that we can do is say *Credo*, I accept. And he said, "The amazing thing is, I yielded, and within three weeks I had such insights into the immorality of artificial birth control." He became one of the champions fighting it. He was the first Catholic thinker in 1930, when the Protestants had the Lambeth Conference and suddenly accepted birth control as valid, he was the first one to oppose it. In 1968, when *Humanae Vitae* was published, he was the first thinker to defend the pope. It is the notion of authority, to submit. An act of intellectual humility: you recognize you are weak, you make mistakes, and you need someone above you who guides you.

Shortly before his death, when he solemnly confided his literary bequest to me, he said, "Take care of all the papers that I've left." But he said, "If you find *one line* which is not in total agreement with the teaching of the Church, do me one favor, burn it." Not many intellectuals would do that. Not many of modern theologians would say, "I submit." It was his joy to submit, because he was submitting to God. And don't forget, he was an extremely powerful man. I was quite conscious throughout my life that I was close to someone who was an intellectual giant, and that I was a little dwarf sitting on his shoulder. All the work that I have accomplished—teaching in the university, in a secular university, the conferences I've given—I owe it all to him, and he owes it all to God.

Marcus: As we were talking about earlier, this change that came about in him was this vertical dimension, the awakening of this vertical dimension in him, which really, when you think about any conversion, that's what it is. There's the awareness, the acceptance and the surrender to this vertical dimension in our life. It really is there all the time, isn't it? We live in a culture that in many ways is blind to that vertical dimension, but also that presents many substitutes for this vertical dimension, imitations. Some very subtle ones. Talk a bit for our audience about what we mean by this vertical dimension in our life.

Alice: It means to see a reality that can only come from above, something that man could never have invented, something that is so overwhelming that it seems to upset at first sight all natural values. For example, take the gospel: "You are to love those who persecute you" (see Matt. 5:44). Now, if you take natural morality and simply say: "Don't do harm to those who harm you …" But to say that you should *love* them? And if someone wants to take your coat, you should you give him your cloak as well? You know that you are rejected and calumnized and people criticize you, and you love them and you thank them?!

If you read the lives of the saints, what is so absolutely amazing is that they had an enormous self-contempt because they discovered themselves to be sinners. And that leads me to my next point concerning my husband. A conversion is something paradoxical, because from one point of view, he was so exalted, he was so happy. He was radiating such joy that the spiritual director, when my husband said to him, "What should I do for Lent?" said, "Not speak about your conversion." Because he couldn't speak about anything else!

Now suppose that you're madly in love and everybody that you see, you speak to about your beloved, and you speak to people who have never loved, and finally they say, "Well, for goodness' sake, stop it now. I've had enough!" People just could not understand that he was in love, that he was totally inebriated by the beauty of God that was revealed through Christ and His Church. This is why when you interviewed Steven Ray and David Currie and both of them exuded such joy I said to myself, "This is exactly what my husband has experienced." On the one hand, this overwhelming joy. And on the other hand, he made the discovery that he was a sinner. You see, up to that time, he had led a good life; he was definitely someone who was kind and good; he had an enormous respect for the sexual sphere, probably because of his love for his mother and his sisters. He had a very, very deep sense for the nobility of femininity, and he could never stand people who looked down upon women; he just found it absolutely horrible. So, you see, he didn't have the obstacles that most people have to finding the faith—because they lead a bad life or that sort of thing. He was an extraordinarily good person. Of course, he was selfish and that sort of thing, but it didn't bother him until now.

Marcus: This finding, and becoming open to, and seeking out the vertical dimension of life reminds me of one of the Beatitudes, "Blessed are those who hunger and thirst for righteousness, for they shall be satisfied" (Matt. 5:6). How does that relate to this conversion in your husband's life?

Alice: Well, as I said, it was like a revelation of a new world. There is some sort of a faint analogy in Plato's *Republic*, book 7, when people live in a dark den, and then, all of a sudden, one of them escapes and sees the sunlight. That was his experience, as I said, the paradox of the joy and simultaneously the discovery: "Goodness, I'm a sinner." The priest who brought him into the Church said, "Don't forget, it's not the Church that needs you; you need the Church." When he had to make his first Confession and examine his life, all of a sudden, he discovered lots of things that he had been blind to. You know, we don't pay much attention to our weakness, but all of a suddenly he focused on it, and he realized, "Goodness, yes, I'm a sinner. God have mercy on me." That is the first lesson of humility. And this was linked to another thing: the joy of conversion, the joy of being God's child, the joy of knowing the Holy Trinity lives in you. That was so overwhelming for him, and he wanted to share it.

And from this moment on, he became a missionary. Missionary, in the sense of saying, "Truth is not *mine*." You know, I taught so many years in a secular world, and my one big problem was relativism. I discovered there were two main obstacles to faith. One of them was to deny the objectivity of truth, and the other was to lead a bad and immoral life. These are the two main obstacles to finding God.

Now, my husband never was a relativist. And I always said to my students, when they would say, "You're just telling us *your* ideas," I would say, "If I say something false, give me the patent of this stupidity. But if I say anything which is true, it is *ours*." Now, this is what *catholic* means: it is universal. And if something is *true*, God exists. Christ is the Son of God Who has saved us. He has founded the Church, which contains the plenitude of revelation. This is a straight line, and my husband discovered it: this is *ours*. And therefore, what he had received, his one great longing was to share it. And in all of his life, about a hundred people, families and friends, converted.

One of the greatest joys he had in the United States was the conversion of a young Jew who was a student of his and, taking his course, was very much impressed by him, just as I was tremendously impressed by his teaching. And one day this young Jew said to him—it was a Jesuit university at Fordham—"You know, the other professors say, 'We're not going to try to force you to become Catholic. We totally respect the fact that you're not. No one is going to try to influence you.'" And my husband stopped in the middle of the street and said, "*What?* That's what they said to you? Well, I tell you, Neil, I'd walk to the end of the world to gain for you the joy of entering the Church." And a few months later, he became a Roman Catholic! He was baptized. He was dating my sister, and I was hoping he would become my brother-in-law. And one very fine day, she came back late at night, and she was sobbing, and she said to me, "Neil told me he has a religious vocation." Well, you cannot fight with God. And, believe it or not, he became a Carthusian monk and founded the first Carthusian monastery in the United States.

We remained in close contact until the very end of his life. And my sister had gone back to Europe and then married someone else since. They hadn't seen each other for thirty-five years. And then three years ago, she came back, and she called him and asked him whether she could see him. And he said, "Yes, I have the permission to see you." He saw her after thirty-five years. He said to me, "I have prayed for her every single day at Holy Mass." And they had a beautiful exchange, and when she left, she said, "Well, it's goodbye. I'll see you in eternity." And he said, "Why? Maybe I'll have the joy of seeing you again." And three months later he was dead. And Fr. Benedict told me that he knew him extremely well. And when I said that I was hoping he would become my brother in-law, he practically fell off his chair!

Marcus: You had mentioned that two of the barriers that stand in the way of people recognizing the presence of God, the voice of God in their life, are relativism and immorality. What else stands in the way? What else prevents people in our culture from recognizing the vertical?

Alice: I do believe, unfortunately, in the United States and in the world at large—but particularly in the Western world, because we are rich, and it's not always a blessing, it's very comfortable, but it's not always a blessing, and from a moral point of view it can be an enormous obstacle—I'm going to say something which is unfortunately true, but in the United States, we have a distorted sense of value, and we are putting what is lower higher and what is higher lower. When you speak to people coming from simple countries and so-called underdeveloped countries, sometimes they have a much better hierarchy of values.

Now, you're going to say that maybe I'm too severe, but it seems to me that if you ask the average American what are the things that he cares for—well, making a fast buck, lots of money, and sports. I just left New York a couple of days ago and it was wild. It's practically a question of life or death if the Mets or the Yankees are going to win. I have nothing against sport, and it is certainly something which is valid, but it is way, way, way down on scale. And we forget that our primary duty is to praise God. That is my glory, that is my title of honor. This is something so tragic, that we are so concerned about making money that we become blind. And of course, when this blindness is particularly apparent in our politicians, to the point that there are certain things they no longer see, the effect on the whole of the country is a disaster. There are two things that are very prevalent in everyone's mind today: the World Series and then the election.

The election is going to be a test: What is the hierarchy of values of the majority of American people? Do they place moral values on top, or do they place economic values on top? Do they place personal interest and personal advantage on top, or do they consider that the first obligation of a country is a moral obligation to exercise justice and to respect the lives of innocent people? If we don't, even though our economic system is booming, even though we have made more money than ever before, even though you know the stocks apparently keep going up, we are doomed.

My husband was so conscious of this. I still recall with tears in my eyes ... He gave hundreds of talks in his life, in seventeen countries, and the last talk that he gave was in March '75 in Orange, California. It was soon after *Roe vs. Wade*, and I recall him saying that a country that legalizes the murder of its own innocent children is *doomed*. And he left the podium. If America, this blessed country that has so many advantages, forgets that the primary duty is a moral obligation to respect innocent life, even though we make money, we are doomed. When you study the history of Rome, you see that Rome was defeated by people that had only clubs and things like that because Rome was morally decadent. And this is what is threatening us today. Our politicians do not lead us upward, and people follow. I remember, my husband cried the last years of his life because of the blindness that was spreading more and more.

Marcus: To come back to your husband's conversion ... We talked about the horizontal joy, the beauties of God's creation and all that your husband experienced, with his knowledge and commitment and understanding of Christ way in the background, which in many ways he was blind to.

And then how through the teaching and friendship of this philosopher professor (Max Scheler) and the spark of God's grace, his life awakened to the presence of the vertical. And then there's the witness of his own sister, until eventually he himself becomes a tremendous witness. Would you say that his book *Transformation in Christ* is one of his greatest books, describing this journey of faith?

Alice: This book changed my life. I met my husband when he was living in a very slummy apartment, very close to Harlem, New York. I was living at the Waldorf Astoria at the time, and the contrast between the two places was really remarkable. Needless to say, I wasn't footing the bills; I was living with an uncle, and we had plenty of money. And he was talking about transformation in Christ ... and you know, he spoke about it in such a sublime way, I assure you, when I left to go back to the Waldorf I was inebriated. I had had a Catholic instruction. I believe that I knew my Faith extremely well. I was a daily communicant. I had an extremely pious father. But the idea that I had to be *transformed*, that I had to be totally renovated, was for me new. It's so amazing that some of the nuns did not make that clear to us. You have to work on yourself; you have to let Christ chisel you. It was an inspiration to me. It was a dimension of my Faith that I just didn't see. I believe personally that *Transformation in Christ* is one of the great books of the twentieth century. I've read it about fifteen times. I reread it recently, and I still discover new gems. But, of course, people will say, "She's prejudiced, because it is her husband's book." But it's actually the opposite. It was through *Transformation in Christ* that I discovered who my husband was.

Caller: It's really an honor to talk to both of you. My question is, did your husband ever run into or talk about Edith Stein?

Alice: Yes, yes indeed. I'm so glad that you're raising the question, because it's something that I wanted to say and I had no time for it. They have the same intellectual background: both of them were brilliant students of Husserl. She was born on the same day, but two years later. She came to Göttingen when my husband had already left. But he had founded the philosophic society, and wherever my husband came there was a lot of movement; everybody knew his name. They had the same admiration for Husserl, the same respect for him. The same admiration for Adolf Reinach, who was one of their favorite teachers. Adolf was killed during the war, shortly after his conversion, in which my husband played a role. He was a liberal Jew, and when he entered the army, my husband sent him the *Confessions* of St. Augustine. He was so responsive to it that my husband immediately sent him a Catholic missal. And shortly afterward, he was killed. But in the meantime, he had been baptized as a Protestant. When he was killed, my husband was asked to say a few words at his burial at Göttingen, and Edith Stein was there. That's the first time he met her. She knew about him, but I don't think he knew about her. He was well-known at Göttingen by all the students. But he said to me that she was so shy and reserved, a typical introvert; and my husband was a typical Italian, he was an extrovert. She was very shy and she answered in monosyllables, and so no contact was established, which afterward made him awfully sad. They met a second time afterward in Salzburg in 1930, when she gave a brilliant talk on feminism and femininity. And once again, she was very, very reserved, very difficult to come close to. Afterward, as more and more he discovered what an extraordinary person she was, he regretted that no contact had been established.

Marcus: For those who may not know who Edith Stein was, she was a Jewish philosopher atheist.

Alice: She was raised as an Orthodox Jew, but she lost her faith when she was a teenager. But she had a love of truth and she was leading a moral life, so she had no obstacles. And when she went to Göttingen, she discovered Max Scheler, and the prejudices were eliminated. And then, she read *The Life of St. Teresa of Ávila*—just as my husband read the life of St. Francis of Assisi—and she discovered the supernatural. She read the *Life*, starting at seven o'clock in the evening, and she stopped reading at seven o'clock in the morning and said, "I'm becoming a Roman Catholic."

Then she was teaching for a while, but no job at the university was possible because she was only a woman, even though she was a most talented woman, as you can imagine. And then she became a nun. Then she had to leave Germany and went to Holland, but as soon as the Dutch bishops condemned Nazism, she was arrested and sent to Auschwitz and died. And she was canonized last year (1998).

There really are a lot of similarities between her and my husband. When you read my book, *The Soul of a Lion*, you're going to see a lot of parallels in the interpretation of Husserl and Heiner.

Marcus: Let's take this email: "Dear Marcus and Dr. von Hildebrand, I read *Transformation in Christ*, a masterpiece with practical application to life. From my observation, it seems that humility is the first, greatest step to true conversion. I've seen it with my husband, as well as with other converts. I tried giving this book to someone who makes a ton of money, lives the high life, but is on a completely self-destructive path. How do you reach someone who has everything: looks, money, intelligence, but is miserable? You can't strip the person of the material things he or she has, but how do you deflate their ego?"

Alice: You can't deflate their ego, but you can pray for them. That's another thing that I want to say which I had no time to say previously, another thing my husband discovered in the Roman Catholic Church: the meaning of sacrifice. I assure you, the word *sacrifice* probably was not in his vocabulary before he converted. It is one of the beautiful things about the Catholic Church. In reality, there is so little we can do for others. We can hurt others easily, but it's very difficult to do good for them. We can hurt them *immediately*, we can only do them good *through God*. And there you have the two unique means that God offers us every day, prayer and sacrifice. Unfortunately, after Vatican II, you will notice the notion of sacrifice has been more and more eliminated. And this is why so many convents have gone downhill, because now you have a cocktail hour replacing discipline, sacrifices, and fasting. Let us reintroduce the greatness of sacrifice; that is a backbone of religious life. Preaching doesn't do it most of the time. Of course, in the case of my husband, there is no doubt about what he called "the apostolate of being." When you radiate peace and love, someone could come to and say, "I'm so unhappy. What is your secret? You are happy, you radiate joy." And then gently and slowly, you can speak about the mystery of God in your soul.

Caller: Can you define the term *reality of the vertical?* I don't know what that means.

Alice: Vertical is Marcus' interpretation of what is meant by supernatural. It means the dimension of reality that cannot be invented by human beings, that is so absolutely superior and transcendent to whatever entered in a man's head. You know, my husband always said one of the most powerful proofs of the divinity of Christ is that He could never have been invented by a human being: someone who is all-powerful and all-good and chooses to be incarnated in the womb of a woman in order to save us. This is something that man has never imagined. You always imagine someone who's lower trying to reach a higher stage. But that someone who is all-perfect would choose to become weak for our sake, this is something overwhelming that can only be divine.

Marcus: The vertical dimension is being touched by God. I was thinking about the vertical, because so much of beautiful traditional Catholic art is to draw our focus upward. And last night, my wife and my sons and I were out having a bonfire in our property and cooking hot dogs late at night, and the stars were so beautiful. We were laying on a rug and looking up. We're drawn upward. What do we see when we're drawn upward? It reminds us of that passage in Romans: "For what can be known about God is plain to them, because God has shown it to them. Ever since the creation of the world his invisible nature, namely, his eternal power and deity, has been clearly perceived in the things that have been made. So they are without excuse; for although they knew God they did not honor him as God or give thanks to him, but they became futile in their thinking and their senseless minds were darkened. Claiming to be wise, they became fools" (Rom. 1:19–22).

Alice: My husband said to me, "After I converted, the music of Beethoven and Mozart, and the greatest of Leonardo, was only more beautiful; it doesn't become less beautiful." And maybe this was best expressed in his relationship and interpretation of love in marriage. He loved his wife very deeply. But the very moment that you see your wife as a temple of God, and divine grace is seen in her and you partake of Christ's love for her, you reach a dimension of beauty which is not conceivable on a purely natural level. So he simply said, "You gain everything and you lose nothing, because everything that you loved before, it's not lost, it's simply more beautiful, it's transfigured." You know, you hear the songs of birds, the singing of birds, and you know they sing of God's grace. So I mean even in moments of severe trial, and when you read this book, you are going to see what he went through, persecuted by the Nazis. He was the enemy number one, sought by the Gestapo ... but nevertheless he still had this supernatural joy: *God loves me.*

Marcus: I just want to clarify, so people who don't understand your presuppositions don't misunderstand you. When you were talking earlier about the struggles that have happened in monasteries and such since Vatican II, you don't mean to criticize Vatican II per se, but the way it's been applied, misinterpreted ...

Alice: Yes, purposely misinterpreted.

Marcus: There really is a call for us, as we know from John Paul II, to read and understand and live the teaching of the Church. There's a challenge to that. Let's take our next email: "Dear Marcus with Dr. von Hildebrand, please relate Dr. Dietrich von Hildebrand's concept of 'value' to the modern aesthetic. How would you place it within the context of what today passes for art?"

Alice: That's a huge topic! You know, my husband has written a two-volume, five-hundred-page work on aesthetics. For him, beauty is not just something that is subjectively satisfying, which gives me pleasure, which is fun. It is something that possesses an objective character. Don't forget, God is Beauty itself; and what is beautiful, in some modest way, reflects God and speaks of him. So therefore, this is why there is a strict obligation for Catholic architects to produce churches that are beautiful. And after Vatican II, for some reason, they started building churches that were *so ugly* that you simply say, well this is built for the devil; it's not built for God. God deserves what is the most beautiful. This way, I'm so grateful about the convent in Hanceville. Mother did not build this magnificent place for the nuns for their enjoyment, but for the glory of God, because it is God's house and nothing can be beautiful enough for God. The question is a very, very good question, but unfortunately I have too little time to answer it in detail.

Marcus: Before we take the email in a moment, there's a text from Psalm 36 that I think addresses this issue of the vertical dimension of God's supernatural voice, in connection with us, His creation. What happens when we're blind to that, because what happens is we can be blind to the voices from within so that we can't discern what's right from wrong.

Alice: You mean deaf of course.

Marcus: Of course, yes, yes, yes. I'm glad you're here to make sure I'm getting my words right. Let's reflect on this word in Psalm 36: "Transgression speaks to the wicked deep in his heart; there is no fear of God before his eyes" (Ps. 36:1). Is this not an expression of someone lost in the horizontal?

Alice: You know, it is a tragic world in which we live, that we've become blind and we've become deaf. And many people choose to, because they just want to live as they please, and by so doing, they become slaves of their pride and their concupiscence. This is why, although we live in a rich society, as Mother Teresa said, we are extremely poor. And sometimes you go to truly poor countries—or so they are called by the developed countries—where people still have a sense of right and wrong. Was it not Isaiah who said, "[They] call evil good and good evil" (Isa. 5:20)? To my joy, a friend of mine, a black man from Ghana, said, "In my country, there's no word for abortion. It doesn't exist in our vocabulary because it doesn't enter into a head that we can kill a child which is being developed in the mystery of its mother's womb."

Marcus: And when we lose track of the vertical voice, of course, then we are losing the discernment. Psalm 36 continues in this way, "For he flatters himself in his own eyes that his iniquity cannot be found out and hated" (Ps. 36:2). If you don't believe in the vertical observation of God, then you don't think what you're doing can be found out. "The words of his mouth are mischief and deceit; he has ceased to act wisely and do good. He plots mischief while on his bed; he sets himself in a way that is not good; he spurns not evil" (Ps. 36:3–4).

But then in Psalm 37, we hear the other side, "Fret not yourself because of the wicked, be not envious of wrongdoers! For they will soon fade like the grass, and wither like the green herb. Trust in the LORD, and do good" (Ps. 37:1–3).

Alice: You know, that was typical of my husband's conversion. Before that, there was a notion of good and evil. The moment he converted, there was a notion of sin. Because sin is against God, and therefore, God alone can forgive sins. The Pharisee says, "You forgive sins. You cannot. God alone can forgive sins." Now, if Christ is not God, they were right. But being God, He could forgive sins. We must understand that every sin offends God. It can hurt another human being, but the offense is to God. And this is what is so prominent in Catholic teaching: the worst thing that you can do is to offend God. And I say, people who go to the polls on the seventh of November should say to themselves, "I want to vote for a candidate who is not going to give priority to what is unimportant and totally neglect what is essential, namely not to commit sins."

Marcus: Why don't we take this last email very quickly? "Dear Marcus and Dr. von Hildebrand, what would you suggest to someone thinking about coming into the Church who has encountered Catholics who seem to contradict each other in their understanding of Church teaching?"

Alice: That's an excellent question and a very easy one to answer. What's so marvelous about the Catholic Church is that there is an authority. There is the official teaching of the

Church that hasn't changed for two thousand years. So don't pay attention to the chattering of people who are going to say this and that. These are *their* opinions. Turn to what the Church has taught: unchanged teaching for the last two thousand years. In spite of the imperfections of some of her leaders, in spite of the fact we've had bad popes, in spite of that, the teaching hasn't changed. And for this we have to be infinitely grateful.

Marcus: Let me ask you finally, now that you've shared the journey of your husband, how has walking beside your husband and experiencing his conversion of faith helped your own lifelong Catholic Faith grow?

Alice: The first time I heard him speaking about the necessity to be transformed, it was absolutely decisive for me. And apart from that, he has given me an understanding of the Mass which is infinitely deeper than what I had before. He has opened for me the incredible beauty of the Catholic liturgy. One of the things that he has taught me, which once again was not so prominent, despite my Catholic education, is the link between Christ and His Bride. He could never separate Christ and the Church. He said to me, "I love the Roman Catholic Church as I love my bride. She is my great love." And many a time, at the end of his life, he was weeping because of what some people would say about the Church. I mean Catholics, making no distinction between the Holy Catholic Church and certain members of the Church who sometimes are particularly miserable.

Marcus: Thank you, Dr. von Hildebrand, for sharing with us your journey and the journey of your husband. It is a great inspiration.

As I thought about what we were to speak on tonight, I was reminded of an image that's helped me understand the importance of both the horizontal and the vertical, and the importance of the balance. It's best expressed by the cross. This happens to be my old preaching cross that was given to me by my parents when I was ordained. You see, most of our culture, of our world, is caught in the horizontal, and the problem with the horizontal focus is that, without the presence of God's voice and His authority in our lives, the tendency of the horizontal is to be inward. Even the best of us — as altruistic as you might be — apart from God, it will all end up being about what is best for me. We may be doing things for others, but ultimately there will always be that core of [selfishness], what is good for me. We see that with our computers. It's all what's good for me, and how to entertain me, empower me, everything for me. And that, to me is, the essence of the horizontal.

But the reaction is sometimes to turn to the vertical, to a relationship with God, but then reject the horizontal. For example, like Christian Science, which would have you believe that none of the horizontal is real and our only focus is to be vertical.

But the reality of the Christian faith is illustrated in the cross, because it is the expression of the Incarnation, of God coming into our world. The vertical *enters* the horizontal and brings glory to the horizontal, as we see in Scripture. In our world, we can see and experience the reality of God, and to me, the image of the cross represents that. The top part of the cross represents God reaching down to us by His grace. The bottom part of the cross, of course, represents our reaching up to God, by His grace enabling us to reach to Him in faith. And then the horizontal arms of the cross are that aspect of our faith that is so necessary and is expressed when we reach out in love to others. Jesus said the two great commandments are to love the Lord your God with all your heart, mind, soul, and strength and to love your neighbor as yourself. That's faith. Not just mind, but heart, mind, soul, and strength. And that's expressed as we reach out to one another.

That is the balance of the vertical in the horizontal that we find in Christ, and that is to be found in our lives. A woman asked what we meant by the vertical. It means sur-render to Christ, accepting His grace and His love, so that by His transformation of our hearts, we can then seek and find Him as He draws us closer to Him. God bless you.